The Story of All Stories

The Story of All Stories

Genesis 1–11

Darrell W. Johnson

REGENT COLLEGE PUBLISHING
Vancouver, British Columbia

Regent College Publishing
5800 University Boulevard
Vancouver, BC V6T 2E4 Canada
www.regentpublishing.com

Regent College Publishing is an imprint of the Regent Bookstore <www.regentbookstore.com>. Views expressed in works published by Regent College Publishing are those of the author and do not necessarily represent the official position of Regent College <www.regent-college.edu>.

ISBN 978-1-57383-569-5

Cataloguing in Publication information is available from Library and Archives Canada.

All Scripture quotations, unless otherwise indicated, are taken from the New American Standard Bible®, copyright 1995 by the Lockman Foundation.

To Sharon
A most excellent helper

Contents

Introduction

"Tell me a story, Grandpa."

Nearly every one of our grandchildren has made that request many times, as did their parents when they were children. "Tell me a story, Daddy." "Tell me a story, Mommy."

"Tell me a story." Not just to entertain, although good stories certainly do that, but to help make sense of our lives, of the mystery of our existence.

We are the creatures who are always seeking to understand who we are, where we are, and how we are supposed to be who we are where we are.

And the primary, indeed, the primal way we do it is by telling stories. Every culture in every era in every part of the world has a story or cluster of stories it passes on to each succeeding generation to help each it navigate the mystery of being human on this earth. In many tribal cultures a "rite of passage" into adulthood is the demonstration that one is able to tell such a story or stories to the satisfaction of the elders. This is still the case today in many parts of Asia, Africa, and the Middle East, because the elders know that we simply cannot make our way in the world without knowing the stories that shape our understanding of the world. All of us—children, parents, and grandparents—need stories that help us know who we are, where we are, and how we are to be who we are where we are.

"Tell me a story."

This is part of the reason, it seems to me, we in the so-called West are presently a people adrift (I say "presently" because I pray that soon this will not be the case). We no longer have a compelling story to tell each other and to pass on to the next generations. Of course, we have all kinds of stories. The bookstore and online sources offer countless stories, and I enjoy reading many of them to our grandchildren or watching many of them on video—*Superman*, *Star Wars*, *Frozen*, to name a few contemporary examples.

As powerful as they are, none of them finally satisfy. All of them are seeking to do what stories are supposed to do, but none of them finally help us make sense of our world.

Thank God there is a story—actually, a cluster of stories—that has served this purpose in the past and can do so again in the present. It is the story that served as the foundation for Western civilization and, sadly, has largely been forgotten by Westerners, at least for now. I am referring, of course, to the story told by the Bible. This is the story I so long for my grandchildren to know, and it appears that the only way they are going to know it is by hearing it from me and from their parents.

You may have a hard time imagining what I am about to tell you. I learned the biblical story/stories in public school! Yes, in Sunday school, but also in public school. Every Christmas season, we actually read through the story as told by Matthew and Luke—in public school! The teachers never overtly argued for the truth of the story, but they did read it. I even learned the great Christmas carols in public school. Every Easter season we actually read the story as told by all four Gospel writers in public school. The teacher talked about the Easter Bunny and other such things, but he or she also said something like, "The Bible claims that a dead man came to life." The same was true of Jewish holidays. Around the time of Passover, we learned about Israel being set free from Egypt, and we read from the book of Exodus. Can you imagine?

This is why, by the way, we were able to go on to university and study art history, for example, and actually "get it." When we saw a painting like Rembrandt's *Return of the Prodigal Son*,[1] we could enter into its reality because we had heard, somewhere along the way, Jesus' great story about the father and his two sons. Today, if we were to take a group of average university students to the great art museums, they probably would not have a clue about how to interpret what is on the walls. If we were to take them to the Sistine Chapel in Rome and have them look up at Michelangelo's masterwork upon the ceiling, most would have no clue as to what he was declaring and, perhaps even more sadly, would not have a clue about the final meaning of life being portrayed on the ceiling.

"Tell me a story."

Thank God, God himself has told a story—a great cluster of stories—in the sixty-six books of the Bible. And the key to the whole story that these sixty-six books tell is the first "half" of the Bible—not the Old Testament, as one might think, but Genesis 1-11, the other half being all of Genesis 12–Revelation 22. The story that begins in Genesis 12 with the call of Abraham and Sarah and then walks through the history of Israel, leading up to the coming of Jesus Christ and finally to the new heavens and the new earth, makes sense when it is heard in the context of the story in Genesis 1-11. The authors of the second half of the Bible assume we know the first half. This means that if our children and grandchildren, our friends and neighbors, are to understand the whole

1. Rembrandt Harmenszoon van Rijn, *Return of the Prodigal Son*, c. 1661-1669, oil on canvas, 262 x 205 cm, Hermitage Museum, St. Petersburg, Russia.

story God tells, we need to make sure they know the story that makes sense of the rest of the story.

Fascinatingly, all the other stories we tell, all the other great stories and myths all cultures tell, are grappling with what Genesis 1–11 reveals. These chapters make sense of all our other stories, for they speak to the fundamental questions we ask in every age:

Where did we come from?

Why are we here?

What are we?

Are we alone in the universe?

What does it mean to be human?

Why does it hurt to be human?

Why can we human beings build impressive skyscrapers, make exquisitely beautiful art, play sports, and compose and sing songs and then use one another for our own ends, manipulate laws, exploit the earth, and kill?

What is wrong with us?

Why do human societies rise and flourish and then begin to rot at the core?

Where is God in all of this?

What kind of God is he in all of this?

Can the world be fixed?

Who will do the fixing?

And when?[2]

2. For a thoughtful examination of the answers that the Old Testament in general, and Genesis in particular, gives to questions like these, I commend to you Iain Provan, *Seriously Dangerous Religion: What the Old Testament Really Says and Why It Matters* (Waco, Tex.: Baylor University Press, 2014).

The most important role of the stories in Genesis 1–11 is to help us realize why we need a Savior and what the Savior comes to do. When we inhabit the stories of Genesis 1–11, we come to realize just how good the gospel of Jesus Christ really is.

"Tell me a story, Grandpa."

So, let us listen to one of our great-great-great-great—on it goes—great-great-great grandpas tell us a story. Tradition says it was Moses. For the sake of simplicity, let us go with that tradition for now, and let us listen to Moses tell us a story.

This is The Story That Makes Sense of All Our Stories.

1

The Creator Creates Creation

Genesis 1:1–2:3

We begin our study of The Story That Makes Sense of Our Stories at the beginning, Genesis 1. [1]

Many people in our cultures are familiar with the show tune "Do-Re-Mi" from the musical *The Sound of Music*.[2] This catchy song gives an introduction to the major musical scale using the solfège system—"do," "re," "mi," and so on—and although it is simple and can easily be memorized by children, it gives the listener a solid foundation for learning and understanding Western music. In a similar way, the concise and memorable Genesis 1 gives

---

1. The chapter and verse numbers are not part of the original text; they were added only eight hundred years ago to facilitate referencing specific texts. The content of Genesis 2:1-3 is not a new section or a new chapter, but is the continuation of Genesis 1. Therefore, whenever I say "Genesis 1," I mean Genesis 1:1–2:3.

2. Richard Rodgers and Oscar Hammerstein II, "Do-Re-Mi," in *The Sound of Music* (Rodgers and Hammerstein, 1959).

a foundation for understanding the Bible and God's work in the world. If only our cultures knew Genesis 1 as well as "Do-Re-Mi"!

Genesis 1, the beginning of The Story That Makes Sense of Our Stories, is a poem. It is not a philosophical treatise, although it opens up profound philosophical insights. Nor is it a scientific paper, although it has huge scientific implications. Genesis 1 is a song.

The first three notes of this song are C, C, C: "Creator creates creation."[3] If we get these three notes correct, we can sing the rest of the story in tune. Without these three notes, it is not possible to make sense of our existence. "In the beginning God created the heavens and the earth" (Gen 1:1): "Creator creates creation." Not just "some power or process somehow did something to cause the emergence of Mother Nature." No, Creator creates creation. However it all happens, Creator creates creation.

My heart breaks for the millions of people in our time who are trying to sing the song of life but do not know the first three notes. My heart especially aches for the millions of children who have never heard how the story begins. The first sentence of the story joyfully declares, "The universe is not an accident, and you are not an accident. There is a Creator, a Person, one as personal as you and me. This Creator, who delights to create, created you and everything around you."

Notice how the song is bracketed:

Genesis 1:1: "the heavens and the earth"
Genesis 2:1: "the heavens and the earth."

---

3. I owe the phrase to Old Testament scholar Walter Brueggemann, *Genesis*, Interpretation: A Bible Commentary for Teaching and Preaching (Atlanta: John Knox, 1982), 17.

The hymn of creation begins and ends with the phrase "the heavens and the earth." This is what scholars call a "merism," a figure of speech that uses contrasting points to express totality. "The heavens and the earth" means "the whole universe." The Creator creates everything that is. The universe did not "just happen," and neither did you or I.

Let me now make a number of observations about Genesis 1. In the spirit of the text, I want us to notice 6 + 1 = 7 observations.

THE CREATOR TELLS US

We know that "Creator creates creation" because the Creator himself told us so. This fundamental affirmation of Genesis 1 is not the result of human reflection on creation; rather, it is the result of revelation by the Creator.

Yes, most humans throughout history have come to the conviction that the created order is the work of some sort of creator. Although those who deny that there is someone or something that made the universe tend to get the headlines in the media, they are in the minority. After all, as the Psalmist declares, "the heavens are telling of the glory of God; / And their expanse is declaring the work of His hands" (Ps 19:1). And the apostle Paul, one of the most brilliant thinkers in history, says in his Letter to the Romans, "For since the creation of the world his [God's] invisible attributes, his eternal power and divine nature, have been clearly seen, being understood through what has been made" (Rom 1:20).

Yet, believing the message of the heavens and the earth and finally getting what the created order inherently declares is not the result of human reflection, but of divine revelation. What Jesus says to the disciple Peter when Peter confesses Jesus to be "the Christ, the Son of the living God" (Matt 16:16), can be said to anyone who believes "Creator creates creation": "Flesh and blood did not reveal this to you, but My Father who is in heaven" (v. 17).

That is why the message of Genesis 1 does not fit with any merely human vision of reality. The human author of Genesis 1 did not sit down one day and, after reflecting for a long time on what he or she could see, deduce that there is a Creator. The human author of Genesis 1 was led to that conviction by the revealing work of the Creator. What the Creator reveals connects with much of what the author and his contemporaries thought, but it goes far beyond what any human being could ever deduce.

Indeed, what the Creator reveals often contradicts what humans deduce, and it therefore corrects these deductions. For many of the contemporaries of the author of Genesis 1, creation came into being as the result of intense struggle between warring gods. For instance, in the Babylonian story *Enuma Elish*, the god Marduk splits the body of the goddess Tiamat and makes the heaven and the earth from the separate parts of her body. Genesis 1 contradicts, and therefore corrects, that human deduction by declaring the good news that the heavens and the earth do not emerge out of a struggle between gods who hate each other, but from the decision of the one God who freely chooses to make the heaven and the earth.

Because it is revelation and not deduction, Genesis 1 will both connect and contradict; it will connect with a culture's attempt to make sense of reality, and it will contradict in order to correct these attempts.

Is this not the case with nearly every other great affirmation of the rest of the story? Is this not especially the case with regard to the gospel of Jesus Christ? A virgin conceives. "Things like that really do not happen," our human worldviews say. The Baby lying in Mary's arms is the Creator come to earth. "No way," other worldviews will say. As Jesus dies on a Roman cross, God and humans are being reconciled, and the way into the holy presence of a holy God is being opened. Who would have ever deduced that? On the Sunday morning after Jesus died, the tomb where he had been laid was empty. Jesus was alive. Death had been defeated. "What? Such things do not happen according to our scientific view of reality." Jesus is coming again and bringing with him a whole new heaven and earth. "This is beyond what any reasonable person can deduce by reflecting on our present reality." Yes, it is. Revelation is like that. It comes to us as contradiction that brings about correction so that we might know the truth that sets us free.

Biblical scholar Sidney Greidanus calls our attention to the narrator of Genesis 1. He writes,

> The narrative reveals an omnipresent narrator who was "present" before any humans were created. He is also omniscient, knowing the thoughts of God, "God saw that it was good," and knowing the deliberations of God, "Let us make humankind in our image (v. 26).[4]

Greidanus makes the observation without comment. But it makes me ask, "So who is this narrator?" And I think I know the answer. Who was present and able to know the mind of God in the beginning? Jesus Christ, the Word, as the apostle John calls him: "In the beginning was the Word, and the Word was with God, and the Word was God" (John 1:1). Yes, on one level, Moses, or one of his students, narrated the revelation of Genesis 1. But on another level, behind Moses, before Moses, and beside Moses, is the Word

---

4. Sidney Greidanus, *Preaching Christ from Genesis: Foundations for Expository Sermons* (Grand Rapids: Eerdmans, 2007), 44-45.

of God himself, revealing what none of us would ever be able to deduce.

We know that "Creator creates creation" because the Creator himself tells us so.

CREATOR CREATES OUT OF NOTHING

Creator creates creation *ex nihilo*, "out of nothing."[5] "In the beginning God created . . ." The word the text uses is the Hebrew verb *bara*: "In the beginning God *bara*-ed . . ."

In Hebrew there are two main verbs translated "create." One is *asah*, most often translated "to make," which generally means to take something that already exists and make something else out of it. In the Hebrew Bible, also called the Old Testament, both humans and God *asah*. We take a tree trunk and make boards out of it, and out of the boards we build a house. We take iron ore out of the ground and from it make tracks for trains. We *asah*, and God also *asah*s; Scripture often refers to God as a potter.

But no human ever *bara*-s. Nowhere in the Hebrew Bible do we find a human being *bara*-ing. Only God can *bara*. Why? Because the verb emphasizes making without analogy, making what has never been before—in short, making something out of nothing, *ex nihilo*.

---

5. For a perspective that sees creation in functional terms rather than material terms, see John H. Walton, *The Lost World of Genesis One: Ancient Cosmology and the Origins Debate* (Downers Grove, Ill.: IVP Academic, 2009), 48. He suggests that the pre-creation state of Genesis 1:2 portrays matter, but not functional existence. "These primeval cosmic waters are the classic form that nonexistence takes in the functionally oriented ancient world."

In Genesis 1 we find *bara* at key turning points in the unfolding revelation. We find it in verse 1, at the very beginning, declaring that the whole of the universe is created "out of nothing," without analogy or precedent. We see it in verse 21, where living creatures, animals, come into existence, *bara*-ed. And it occurs in verse 27, where human beings come into existence—three times, *bara*. It is the text's way of saying, "Now get this!" God *bara*-ed humans in his own image; in the image of God He *bara*-ed them; male and female He *bara*-ed them.

Talk about contradicting to correct! At the time Genesis 1 was composed, the song spoke a message that was radically different from messages in the surrounding world, and the same is true today. When the Creator created the universe, there was nothing, and out of nothing God called forth the heavens and the earth. When the Creator created living creatures, the animals, he did so out of nothing. Yes, they are chemically related to what was created before them, but the Creator brought them forth as a new work of creation. And when the Creator created human beings, he did so out of nothing. Yes, we are chemically and biologically related to what came before us, but the Creator brought us forth as a new work of creation. Whatever else we believe about how humans came into being, Genesis 1 calls us to believe that we are *bara*-ed, made without analogy as an unprecedented work. Our contemporaries need to hear this message. You are *bara*-ed, and only God *bara*-s. No one else could have made you. No process, however creative, could have made you. You are the unique work of the Creator, who can bring life out of nothing.

CREATOR CREATES BY SPEAKING

The third observation is that the Creator creates creation by speaking. In Genesis 2 we will find God getting down in the dust to fashion the first human. But what Genesis 1 wants us to know is that God creates by his word. Not by wrestling with primordial powers, not by exerting energy against resistant forces, but simply by speaking. "Let there be" occurs seven times:

"Let there be light" (v. 3).
"Let there be an expanse" (v. 6).
"Let the waters . . . be gathered" (v. 9).
"Let the dry land appear" (v. 9).
"Let the earth sprout vegetation" (v. 11).
"Let there be lights in the expanse" (v. 14).
"Let the waters teem with swarms of living creatures" (v. 20).
"Let the earth bring forth living creatures after their kind" (v. 24).

Seven times, "Let there be." And then an eighth time: "Let Us make man [humanity] in Our image" (v. 26). The Creator creates simply by speaking. Are we surprised, then, that when the Creator comes to earth as one of us, Jesus redeems and re-creates simply by speaking? "Get up, pick up your pallet and walk" (John 5:8). "Be quiet, and come out him[, demon]!" (Mark1:25; see also Luke 4:35). "Hush, be still[, wind and waves]" (Mark 4:39). "Lazarus, come forth" (John 11:43).

This gives us tremendous hope. The God who made us need only speak to make things happen. And he is speaking all the time, speaking into being new creatures in Jesus Christ. One day he will say the word "now," and the new heaven and the new earth will descend.

But I am getting ahead of the text before us.

CREATOR CREATES IN DIVINE TIME

The Creator creates creation in divine time. To put it another way, God acts according to his own timetable. This is the point of the 6 + 1 structure of Genesis 1. Six days plus one equals seven. In the Bible the number seven points to completion or perfection. In the Revelation of Jesus Christ, John speaks of seven Spirits of God (Rev 1:4). John knows there is only one Spirit of God! "Seven Spirits of God" is his way of saying "the Spirit of God in all his completeness, in all his perfection." The seven-day structure of Genesis 1 is a way of saying, "God made the universe and all things within it in his time, according to his perfect schedule."[6]

Genesis 1 is riddled with sevens, not just seven days. For example:

> In verse 1 there are 7 words.
> In verse 2 there are 14 words, 7 x 2.
> In the section about the seventh day, there are 35 words, 7 x 5.

Each noun in verse 1 is repeated by some multiple of 7:

> "God" (*Elohim*): 35 times, 7 x 5.
> "Heaven": 21 times, 7 x 3.
> "Earth": 21 times, 7 x 3.
> "It was good": 7 times.

This is all a way of saying, "However the Creator did it, he did it in his own time."

6. Walton argues that creation in Genesis 1 is portrayed as God's temple. He claims that the seven days allude to the inauguration of a temple, which he says is well attested in the ancient Near East as taking place over a seven-day period and is seen in the inauguration of Solomon's temple (1 Kgs 8:65; 2 Chron 7:9). Ibid., 71-106.

CREATOR CREATES IN A DIVINE WAY

The fifth observation is that the Creator creates creation in a divine way. This is crucial to observe. Look at Genesis 1:2: "The earth was formless and void," in Hebrew *tohu* and *bohu*. *Tohu* means "formless," "without structure," and *bohu* means "void," "empty." The song of creation then sings of how the Creator brings form out of formlessness and fullness out of emptiness. It is beautiful to watch this unfold!

Genesis 1 is laid out in two rows: days one to three and days four to six.

Day One	Day Two	Day Three
Day Four	Day Five	Day Six

In days one to three, we have the movement from formless to form, from chaos to order.

Day One formless	*Day Two* →	*Day Three* form

In days four to six, we have the movement from emptiness to fullness. If you will, in days one to three, God builds the house; in days four to six, God furnishes it.

Day Four void	*Day Five* →	*Day Six* fullness

In day one God calls forth light, the fundamental energy of life. In day two God calls forth the sky to separate the waters. In day three God calls forth the dry land and gathers the waters around it, and God empowers the land to produce vegetation, the support system for the life yet to emerge.

Day One light	*Day Two* firmament	*Day Three* dry land vegetation

Observe carefully what happens next. In day four God goes back, so to speak, to the work of day one and calls forth "lights" that use the existing light. God creates "the cosmic system," as one scholar calls it, that makes for the orderly movement of day and night.[7]

Note, by the way, that the song does not call the sun "the sun," nor the moon "the moon," but just calls them "the greater light" and "the lesser light." Why? The song is speaking a liberating word to the ancient cosmologists who made the sun and the moon into gods, understandably so, given the energy pouring out of the sun every second. I understand the temptation to deify the sun. Yet, it is not a god, but is rather a magnificent light spoken into being by a magnificent Person.

In day five God goes back to the work of day two, and he calls forth fish to live in the waters and birds to live in the sky. God empowers the fish and the birds to reproduce and blesses them to "be fruitful and multiply" (1:22). The Creator revealed in Genesis 1 loves to bless fish and birds!

7. Meredith G. Kline, "Genesis," in *The New Bible Commentary*, ed. D. Guthrie and J. A. Motyer, (Grand Rapids: Eerdmans, 1970), 82.

In day six God goes back to the work of day three and calls forth living creatures to live on the earth and humans to eat the vegetation. God also gives the living creatures the capacity to reproduce. And God blesses human beings to "be fruitful and multiply" (v. 28). The Creator seems to delight in fruitfulness. God loves to see things multiply![8]

Day One light	*Day Two* firmament	*Day Three* dry land vegetation
Day Four lights	*Day Five* birds fish	*Day Six* living creatures human beings

I think you can see, then, that Genesis 1 is not emphasizing six days of creation. I have no doubt that the Creator has the capacity to create in six days, but that is not what the text is emphasizing. After all, when the author of Genesis refers again to God's creative work, he will say "in *the* day when God created" (Gen 5:1; see also 2:4), not the six days. This song is emphasizing the twofold movement from formless to form, from emptiness to fullness.

The text wants us to understand that this is God's way in the world. However long it took (and however long it takes), the Creator loves to move things from chaos to order, from void to fullness.

8. Andy Crouch, *Playing God: Redeeming the Gift of Power* (Downers Grove, Ill.: IVP, 2013), 33, has a wonderful analysis of "teeming" and how God delights in it. In it he writes that God's blessing does not merely produce a numbered or bland fruitfulness, but rather "teeming"—innumerable and creative—fruitfulness.

This is what explains the human longing for order and the human longing for fullness. This is why the gospel of Jesus Christ is full of the words "full" and "fullness." The God who creates is at work bringing order out of the mess and fullness out of the emptiness. [9]

CREATOR CREATES GOOD

The Creator creates a creation that is good; seven times the text says that "it was good." It does not always feel that way now, and Genesis 2–11 will help us understand why.

> Day one: "It was good."
> Day two: No "it was good" statement. Why not? I am not sure. Not because the sky is not good! Maybe, as Bruce Waltke says tongue in cheek, "even God does not say that Mondays are good!"[10]
> Day three: "It was good." It is stated twice, perhaps to make up for its absence on day two.
> Day four: "It was good."
> Day five: "It was good."
> Day six: "It was good." The Creator likes what he is calling forth. The text also says that on day six "it was *very* good," which in

---

9. Walter Brueggemann, *Theology of the Old Testament* (Minneapolis: Augsburg Fortress, 1997), 207, helpfully comments, "The God who creates is the one who can transform any circumstance of chaos into an ordered context where fruitfulness, blessing, prosperity, and well-being are obtainable. The verbs of creation refuse to accept as a given any situation of death and disorder." He also notes that the verb *bara* is particularly prevalent in Isaiah 40-66, a context of exile and despair where God continues to create (*bara*) (149-151).

10. Bruce K. Waltke and Cathi J. Fredricks, *Genesis: A Commentary* (Grand Rapids: Zondervan, 2001), 62.

Hebrew is *tov meʾod*. Why now "very good" rather than just "good"? Because we are made! It is when the creature that God calls "man" and "woman" comes forth that God says "very good."

CREATOR CREATES IN HIS IMAGE

This brings me to my seventh observation. The Creator creates a creature in his own image. The Creator creates a creature who shows the rest of creation who the Creator is and what he is like. This we will examine in more detail in the next chapter.

2

The Glory of Being Human

Genesis 1:1–2:3

Just before the dawn of the twenty-first century, researchers John Naisbitt and Patricia Aburdene wrote a book titled *Megatrends 2000*. They were building on their 1983 bestseller *Megatrends*, which many had touted as a field guide to the future. So as the advent of a new century approached, they put their expertise to work to articulate the trends they predicted would shape the future. The "Millennial Megatrends," as they called them, were:

The Booming Global Economy of the 1990s
A Renaissance in the Arts
The Emergence of Free-Market Socialism
Global Lifestyles and Cultural Nationalism
The Privatization of the Welfare State
The Rise of the Pacific Rim
The Decade of Women in Leadership
The Age of Biology

The Religious Revival of the New Millennium
The Triumph of the Individual[1]

Naisbitt and Aburdene then made this amazing statement: "The most exciting breakthroughs of the 21st century will occur not because of technology but because of an expanding concept of what it means to be human."[2] They maintained that the most important question for the twenty-first century would be "What does it mean to be human?"

Every culture in every age has some kind of story to help make sense of human existence. Each of these metanarratives is asking and answering fundamental questions. I have suggested that the struggles our cultures are presently facing are a result of having no compelling narrative. There are many narratives being offered, but there is no single larger story to make sense of these smaller stories.

This is what makes Genesis 1–11 such a great gift. Here is a story that, when given a chance to make its case, begins to put things into perspective. The story spoke a liberating word to those who first heard it centuries ago, and it speaks a liberating word to those who hear it in our century. We finally begin to understand the glory of being human, for as we make our way through Genesis 1–11, we begin to discover why Jesus Christ needed to come into our world and what he came to do. Indeed, as we work through the story, we are led to the feet of Jesus, who turns out to be all we were originally made to be.

1. John Naisbitt and Patricia Aburdene, *Megatrends 2000: Ten New Directions for the 1990's* (New York: William Morrow, 1990), 13.
2. Ibid., 16.

In the last chapter, I suggested that the main affirmation of Genesis 1 is, in the words of Old Testament scholar Walter Brueggemann, "Creator creates creation," and I offered seven observations on what the song is singing. We are going to linger awhile on the seventh observation: Creator creates a creature in his own image. "Let Us make man [humankind] in Our image, according to Our likeness. . . . God [bara-ed] man [humankind] in His own image, in the image of God He [bara-ed] him, male and female He [bara-ed] them" (1:26–27).

PERSONAL CONTEXT

Let us step back from the text for a few minutes and speak to the larger context in which we have to come to terms with this passage. Like you and every other human being alive today, I do not read Genesis 1 in a vacuum. Like you, I read "Let us make man [humanity] in our image" in the context of multiple ever-conflicting claims about what it means to be human.

I grew up in the world of science. The formative years of my life, from kindergarten through grade seven, were lived in Los Alamos, New Mexico, a small city tucked away in the mountains about fifty kilometers northwest of Santa Fe. Los Alamos is the city where the atomic and hydrogen bombs were designed. When my family first moved there, it was a "closed city"; everyone had to have a top-secret clearance pass to get in and out. All our mail was simply addressed to "P.O. Box 1663, Santa Fe, New Mexico." My youngest brother was born in Los Alamos, but his birth certificate says "P.O. Box 1663, Santa Fe."

Los Alamos was run by the University of California on behalf of the U.S. National Research laboratories. My father was doing physics for the lab, at first working on the design and tests of nuclear weapons, both fission and fusion, both atomic and hydrogen.

He witnessed the explosion of the second hydrogen bomb in the Enewetak Atoll in the South Pacific—an "awe-ful" experience, as he put it, that he prayed no one would ever witness again. He was part of a team of scientists that taught the bulky first computers to think in two dimensions. He himself designed the first computer program to think in three dimensions.

Being the oldest son in a Swedish family meant that I was expected to follow in my father's footsteps. So I too took up physics and mathematics, earning my undergraduate degree in both subjects at the University of California, San Diego, which was designed to be the premier physics institute in the world. I had lectures in theoretical physics from professors like Edward Teller, father of the hydrogen bomb. I had lectures in microbiology with professors like Jonas Salk, inventor of the polio vaccine that bears his name. I took "Philosophy of Science" from Thomas Kuhn, who wrote the influential book *The Structure of Scientific Revolutions*.

During my third year in university, I began to wrestle with a call to the preaching ministry. On April 4, 1968, the night Martin Luther King Jr. was murdered, I gave in to the call. The next week I ventured out to tell my professor of thermodynamics that I was thinking of leaving physics to go to seminary to prepare to preach Jesus and his gospel. He was shocked and disappointed and asked me, "Why would you throw away your brains and a promising future to preach Jesus?"

LEVELS OF MEANING

The person who helped me the most in integrating what I was reading in the Bible with what I was learning in university, especially when it came to the question of what it means to be human, was Richard Bube. When I first met him, he was professor of material sciences and electrical engineering at Stanford University.

In his field he is known for books like *Electrons in Solids, Photoelectronic Properties of Semiconductors*, and other light bedtime reading! In 1971 Bube wrote a book entitled *The Human Quest*. His central thesis is that reality, and human beings within reality, have to be studied and understood on many different levels and from many different angles. He puts the thesis this way: "There are many levels at which a given situation can be described. An exhaustive description on one level does not preclude meaningful descriptions on other levels."[3]

Bube takes as an example the sentence "I love you." "I love you" can be described on many different levels.[4] For instance, there is the numerical level. There are eight letters in the sentence: I, L, O, V, E, Y, O, U. One letter is repeated, the letter O. The letters are the fifth, ninth, twelfth, fifteenth, twenty-first, and twenty-fifth of the English alphabet, arranged in this order: 9, 12-15-22-5, 25-15-21. This is a true and exhaustive description of the sentence on one level.

But there is also the phonetic level, the level of sound. We have in the sentence a long I, the liquid consonant L, a short O, the voiced fricative V, the silent E, the palatal semi-vowel Y, and the diphthong OU. This too is a true and exhaustive description of the sentence—on one level. And then there is the vocabulary level, the level of words. The letters and sounds interact to form words, and the words point to realities beyond themselves. And then there is the grammatical level. There is a subject (I), a verb (love), and an object (you). The verb is in the present tense. This too is a true and exhaustive description of the sentence—on one level.

---

3. Richard H. Bube, *The Human Quest: A New Look at Science and the Christian Faith* (Waco, Tex.: Word, 1971), 26, 135-136.
4. Ibid., 30-33.

And on it goes to more and more levels, finally to the performative level, when the letters, sounds, words, and grammar make something happen. The sentence "I love you" moves the heart of the person to whom the sentence is spoken.

The thesis again: "There are many levels at which a given situation can be described. An exhaustive description on one level does not preclude meaningful descriptions on another level."[5] Indeed, a complete description of any given situation requires description on every level.

Reality—the universe and we human beings with it—has to be studied and understood on many different levels. These levels include theology, sociology, psychology, anthropology, zoology, botany, biology, chemistry, physics, and origins. We do not finally understand the world or ourselves until we take into consideration descriptions of reality from all these levels. Physicists are right: we are complex packets of mysterious interacting energy forces. But that is not all we are. Chemists are right: Atomic and subatomic particles and waves interact to form molecules and nonliving matter. We are complex chemical machines. But that is not all we are. Biologists are right: Chemicals interact and combine to form more complex forms of life. We are complex cellular computers. But that is not all we are. Botanists and zoologists can describe us and our world further. Anthropologists and psychologists can tell us even more about ourselves. Sociologists can add still more insight. And the theologians then relate it all to ultimate reality, to the Maker, Upholder, and Redeemer of the whole scheme of creation.

Again, a complete description of reality on one level does not preclude a complete description on another level. A complete biological description of the human being, for instance, does not

5. Ibid., 26, 135-136.

do away with the need for a theological description of the human being. And a complete theological description does not do away with the need for a biological description of the human being. The problem emerges when one level thinks it knows the whole, when it ignores the insights of the other levels.

simultaneously

IN THE IMAGE OF GOD

We now come back to the Genesis text: "In the beginning God created the heavens and the earth." (1:1). "Then God said, 'Let Us make man [humankind] in Our image, according to Our likeness'" (v. 26).

Up to this point in Genesis 1, we have heard the Creator say, "Let there be": "Let there be light" (v. 3). "Let there be an expanse" (v. 6). "Let the earth sprout vegetation" (v. 11). But when it comes to the creation of human beings, the wording changes; God gets more personally involved. "Let Us make man [humankind] in Our image, according to Our likeness."

It is this level of understanding that our cultures are dying to know. The universe is not an accident. You are not an accident. Indeed, you are so much more than you know; you are a creature created in the image and likeness of the Creator. Whole books have been written on this text, and rightly so. "In Our image, according to Our likeness." There does not appear to be any significant distinction between the terms "image" and "likeness." In the rest of Scripture they are used interchangeably: in one place, "image," in another, "likeness."

As I read the text, two main facts about being human are being declared: representation and reflection. Human beings are created to represent the Creator in the world and to reflect the nature and character of the Creator in the world.

Representation. In the ancient Near East, when kings and emperors overcame new territories, they would set up an image, or likeness, of themselves to signify their sovereignty over the land and its people. Some kings and emperors still do this. The image, usually in the form of a statue, was the emperor's way of representing himself; it was a visible way to declare an ordinarily invisible fact. The image in some way represented the presence of the emperor.[6] Indeed, the image somehow functioned "as ruler in the place" of the emperor.[7]

Do you see what Genesis 1 is revealing about us? It is something we never would have deduced on our own: God has made us to be his representatives in his creation, a kind of visible expression of an invisible reality.[8] Are we then surprised that God says to us, "Fill the earth, and subdue it; and rule over . . ." (Gen 1:28)? As Ian Hart puts it, "the text is saying that exercising royal dominion over the earth as God's representative is the basic purpose for which God created" men and women.[9] On the creator's behalf, as his representatives we look after the creation. To care for the earth as the creator cares—that is the key. To have dominion, to exercise care over it in the same way the Creator does. "The LORD is good to all, and His mercies are over all His works" (Ps 145:9). That is the spirit

---

6. Waltke and Fredricks, *Genesis*, 65-66.

7. Ibid., 66.

8. Christopher Wright observes that in the new creation humans will again be God's representatives on earth in a kingly and priestly function. "You have made them to be a kingdom and priests to our God; and they will reign upon the earth" (Rev 5:10). Christopher J. H. Wright, *The Mission of God: Unlocking The Bible's Grand Narrative* (Downers Grove, Ill.: InterVarsity, 2006), 415.

9. Ian Hart, "Genesis 1:1–2:3 as a Prologue to the Book of Genesis," *Tyndale Bulletin* 46/2 (1995): 322.

in which we are to exercise our human dignity in the created order, with compassion over all he has made.

Sadly, something has gone wrong with the Creator's image, as we will understand from Genesis 3. The creature, created to care as the Creator cares, does not now practice this. Toward the end of his life, my dad lamented his role in the designing of nuclear weapons. We were created to represent the Creator's concern in the created order. This is part of the glory of being human.

Reflection. As the image and likeness of the Creator, we were created to reflect the Creator's nature and character. Imagine that! The rest of creation is to look at the human species and see the nature and character of God.

In Genesis 5:3 we read that Adam became a father again after losing Abel and Cain. The text says, "He became the father of a son in his own likeness, according to his image." Adam's son Seth somehow reflects the nature and character of Adam and Eve, and somehow we reflect the nature and character of God to one another and to the rest of creation. At one level we are a copy of our Maker.[10]

What do we reflect? Obviously, there is no way we can reflect everything about God's nature and character. We are, after all, finite creatures, so there is no way we can fully reflect the nature and character of the infinite Creator. We are not, and never will be, all-knowing, all-powerful, ever-present—though some of us try to be!

So, what about God do we reflect? We reflect the capacity to create. We reflect the capacity to conceptualize; in Genesis 2 Adam names the animals, reflecting the ability to sort out the diversity of

---

10. John Piper, "The Image of God: An Approach from Biblical and Systematic Theology," *Studia Biblica et Theologica* 1/1 (1971): 15-32.

creation and put things into categories. We reflect the capacity to communicate; we are the creatures who can verbalize, expressing reality in words. This is no small miracle. We reflect the capacity to discern, to make moral judgments, though, as we all painfully know, that capacity has been damaged, in some cases severely so. We reflect the capacity to care. Of all the creatures on earth, we, like God, can put ourselves in others' shoes and feel what they feel.

RELATIONALITY

Take careful note of the wording in the Genesis text. "Let Us," "in Our image," "according to Our likeness." It would seem that the major thing about God we were created to reflect is the "us-ness" of God.

From the beginning of the story, we meet a God who can use the plural pronoun. Indeed, the word for God in Hebrew (*Elohim*) is a plural noun, but it is always used with a singular verb. The God who creates us is the God who speaks of himself as "us."

Yes, the "us" could be the so-called royal "we," which Queen Elizabeth II uses when she says "we" while really meaning "I." The "us" could also refer to the heavenly court, to the angelic hosts that surround the Creator (see Job 1, Isa 6, 1 Kgs 22), but nowhere in the rest of the Bible is it said that we are created in the image and likeness of angels.

God's use of "us" and "our" points to the mystery: within the one God there is somehow a plurality. The living God is not a solitary monad; the living God is a community. It was the Swiss theologian Karl Barth who emphasized this in the last century. "In God's own sphere and being," wrote Barth, "there exists a divine and therefore self-grounded prototype to which this being can

mormonism

correspond."[11] "In God's own being and sphere there is a counterpart: a genuine but harmonious self-encounter and self-discovery; a free co-existence and co-operation; an open confrontation and reciprocity."[12] The living God is Being-in-fellowship. There is an I-thou interchange within the one God—"us," "our," "we." The Genesis text is not overtly speaking of it, but it is opening the door to what would later be understood as the Trinity.

The point of the Genesis text is that we have been created to reflect the relational nature of the Creator. We have been created to reflect the I-thou relationship of the one God. To put it more simply, humanity in the image of the Creator is humanity-in-relationship. God is relationship, and we have been created to reflect that relationship-ness. Simon and Garfunkel used to sing a song with the refrain "I am a rock; I am an island."[13] That is not humanity in the image of God. It is inhumanity. We were made for relationship, which is why broken relationships hurt more than broken bones.

"Let Us make man." We were made to reflect the us-ness of the Creator. We were made for relationship. We were made for relationship with the God who is Relationship. We were made by the Relationship ("us") for the Relationship ("us"). We were made to enjoy relationship with the Relationship. Indeed, as the story will further reveal as it unfolds, we were made to share in the Relationship. We were made to enter into and live with the "us-ness" of God. We were made *by* the Relationship, *for* the Relationship, to live *in* the Relationship. This means we finally know who we are

---

11. Karl Barth, *Church Dogmatics 3/2: The Doctrine of Creation*, ed. G. W. Bromiley and T. F. Torrance (trans. J. W. Edwards, O. Bussey, and H. Knight; Edinburgh: T&T Clark, 1958), 183.

12. Ibid., 185.

13. Simon and Garfunkel, "I Am a Rock," written by Paul Simon, track 5 on side 2 of *Sounds of Silence*, CBS WKCS 9269, 1965, LP.

when we know the Relationship. We finally know what it means to be human when we know the One who made us in his image.

SABBATICAL CREATURES

This brings us to a final observation about what the Creator reveals in Genesis 1: the Creator creates us as sabbatical creatures. This is another truth we never would have deduced on our own. We humans are not the apex of creation; the apex is the Sabbath. God has built into the very fabric of the created order a special day, the seventh day.

Have you ever noticed that in the song of creation the seventh day does not end?

> "And there was evening and there was morning, one day" (v. 5).
> "And there was evening and there was morning, a second day" (v. 8).
> "There was evening and there was morning, a third day" (v. 13).
> "There was evening and there was morning, a fourth day" (v. 19).
> "There was evening and there was morning, a fifth day" (v. 23).
> "And there was evening and there was morning, a sixth day" (v. 31).

But there is no "And there was evening and morning, a seventh day." Day seven does not end. Day seven is the reason the Creator creates: for us to enjoy what the Creator has made and to enjoy the Creator.

You see, in Genesis 1, although we watch God in boundless energy and creativity calling forth light and stars and fruit trees and sea monsters, there is more to God than what is revealed in all that work. This is how Ronald Wallace expresses it:

> That "the Lord rested the seventh day" means that He has not allowed the activity of the days of creation to exhaust him or bind Him, and has limited creation purposely. He has something to say

that could not be said in the work of the six days, something to give that is not yet given through all the enthusiasm and wealth He has put into the world in creating it. . . . God, has therefore something new and something extra to give this world over and above what He has already given it in its creation.[14]

Wow! On the Sabbath day God gives us that which he does not give in all the creativity of creating creation. Wallace has God say,

> I will put a Sabbath day at the heart of the order of things in this universe, and I will bless this Sabbath day weekly as it comes round, and on this day I will communicate to man My own Sabbath rest. On this day I will truly share with him that in Myself which I have kept back so far from creation. . . . Listen to Me as I draw near to speak, and respond to Me as I draw near to offer you my fellowship and seek this day to draw you to Myself.[15]

We were created *by* the Relationship, *for* the Relationship, to live *in* the Relationship.

In the beginning God created us, and God said, "Let Us make man [humankind] in Our image." This is what Jesus Christ comes into the world to make happen. He is the image and likeness of God in every way, and he says to us, "Come to me, all who are weary and have over-burdened yourselves, and I will rest you. I will bring you back into that for which we made you" (adapted from Matt 11:28).

14. Ronald Wallace, *The Ten Commandments: A Study of Ethical Freedom* (Eugene, Ore.: Wipf & Stock, 1998), 66.
15. Ibid., 67-68.

3

Fourfold Relational Harmony

Genesis 2:4–25

A number of years ago, Father John Powell, a popular priest-psychologist, wrote a very helpful little book entitled *Fully Human, Fully Alive*. He builds on a theological conviction first articulated by Irenaeus of Lyons in the second century: "For the glory of God is a living man [human]; and the life of man consists in beholding God."[1]

Powell makes the observation that "true and full human living is based on three components, like the legs of a tripod: intrapersonal dynamics, interpersonal relationships, and a frame of refer-

---

1. Irenaeus, *Against Heresies* 4.20.7, in *The Ante-Nicene Fathers: Translations of the Fathers Down to A.D. 325*, Vol. 1, ed. Alexander Roberts and James Donaldson, rev. A. Cleveland Coxe, American repr. of the Edinburgh ed. (Repr., Edinburgh: T&T Clark; Grand Rapids: Eerdmans, 1989), 490.

ence."[2] What Powell calls "frame of reference" he later calls "vision of reality"; others use the terms "worldview" or "narrative." Powell says,

> Through the eyes of our minds you and I look out at reality (ourselves, other people, life, the world, and God). However, we see these things differently. Your vision of reality is not mine, and conversely, mine is not yours. Both of our visions are limited and inadequate, but not to the same extent. We have both misinterpreted and distorted reality, but in different ways. We have each seen something of the available truth and beauty to which the other has been blind.[3]

He got it right, did he not? That is how it is. Then Powell says,

> The main point is that it is the dimensions and clarity of this vision that determine the dimensions of our worlds and the quality of our lives. To the extent that we are blind or have distorted reality, our lives and our happiness have been diminished. Consequently, if we are to change—to grow—there must first be a change in this basic vision, or perception of reality.[4]

The apostle Paul exhorts us, "Do not be conformed to this world but be transformed by the renewing of your mind" (Rom 12:2), or, as it is rendered in the J. B. Phillips translation, "Do not let the world around you squeeze you into its own mould, but let God re-mould your minds from within." "It is the dimensions and clarity of [our] vision that determine the dimensions of our worlds

---

2. John Powell, *Fully Human, Fully Alive: A New Life Through a New Vision* (Niles, Ill.: Argus, 1976), 10.
3. Ibid.
4. Ibid.

and the quality of our lives." If we are to grow, there must be a change in the vision, a clarification and expansion of our perception of reality.

This is why we are spending time in Genesis 1–11. In these opening chapters of the Bible, we have The Story That Makes Sense of Our Stories. In Genesis 1–11, we see what and who we were created to be. In these chapters, we hear the life-giving news that the universe did not "just happen," and that we humans within it did not "just happen." We were created. Someone wanted us to happen, and Someone chose for us to happen. And in that Someone's goodness, he then tells us a story, a story that puts things into perspective. This story helps us understand the glory of being human, why we do not now have that glory, and how the glory is recovered.

There is no other story in all of literature—ancient, modern, postmodern—like the story told in Genesis 2. For here we are given an expansive picture of what it means to be "fully human, fully alive."

THE STORY ADVANCES

Notice how the story is introduced. There is a shift in the phraseology, signaling a major change in perspective: "This is the account of the heavens and the earth when they were created, in the day that the LORD God made earth and heaven" (Gen 2:4). The first half of the sentence refers to "the heavens and the earth," but the second refers to "earth and heaven." "The heavens and the earth" is the perspective of chapter 1, the perspective of the song before the story; "earth and heaven" is the perspective of chapter 2. "Heaven and earth" (ch. 1) is the vision "from above," so to speak; "earth and heaven" (ch. 2) is the vision "from below." In chapter 1 God is "up," so to speak, sovereign over the work of creation;

in chapter 2 God is "down," intimately engaged in the work of creation. In chapter 1, God creates simply by speaking from the throne; in chapter 2, he creates by hands-on involvement on the ground.

Thus, in Genesis 2, we find the living God being portrayed in bold anthropomorphisms. God portrays himself in human forms. In Genesis 2, God is a potter, forming Adam out of the dust. God is a respiratory technician, breathing into Adam's nostrils. God is a gardener, planting trees that are good for food and pleasing to the eye. God is a farmer, a rancher, shaping animals in unimaginable diversity. God is an anesthesiologist and the master plastic surgeon, shaping out of the man's rib a woman, the most exquisite of all his works.

Notice also the phrase "This is the account of the heavens and the earth" (2:4). Literally it is "These are the generations of . . ." The phrase is used ten times in the book of Genesis. "These are the generations of . . ."

"the heavens and the earth" (2:4)
"Adam" (5:1)
"Noah"
"Shem, Ham, Japheth" (10:1)
"Shem" (11:10)
"Terah" (11:27)
"Ishmael, Abraham's son" (25:12)
"Isaac, Abraham's son" (25:19)
"Esau" (36:1; 36:9)
"Jacob"

Here is why it is important to take note of the phrase: It is not simply a way of saying, "We are going on to another chapter." Rather, it is a way of saying, "We are now going to take things a bit further," or, "Here is a more full development of the story of . . ."[5] In Genesis 2:4, "These are the generations of" is a way of saying, as Sidney Greidanus puts it, "This is what happened to the universe after God created everything 'very good.'"[6]

This means that in Genesis 2 we have a story that shows us in greater detail why God calls the creation "very good." In Genesis 2 we have in pictographic form what God means by "very good." In particular we have fleshed out for us what it means for humans to be created in the image of God. In Genesis 1 we hear, "Then God said, 'Let Us make man [humankind] in Our image, according to Our likeness'" (v. 26). In Genesis 2 we see, in almost childlike simplicity, what it means to be a creature created in the image of the Creator.

In the last chapter, we saw how the words "image" and "likeness" speak of the glory of being human. We mere creatures are placed into the world, into God's garden, as visible representations of an ordinarily invisible reality. We are created to reflect the nature and character of the Creator in and to the world. The rest of creation is to look at us and see something of God's nature and character.

What about God's nature and character are we created to reflect?

> The capacity to create.
> The capacity to categorize.
> The capacity to conceptualize.
> The capacity to communicate.

---

5. David J. Atkinson, *The Message of Genesis 1-11* (Leicester, U.K.: IVP Academic, 1990), 54.

6. Greidanus, *Preaching Christ from Genesis*, 62.

The capacity to care.
The capacity to discern and to decide.

Oh that we would live out these capacities to their fullest! But we are especially meant to reflect the relational nature of God. The living God is a Community, a Fellowship. At the center of all things is a Relationship, and we were made *by* the Relationship, *for* the Relationship, to live *in* relationship. This is the most fundamental thing the Scriptures tell us about being human. In Genesis 2, the God who can say "us" portrays for us the relationship for which he created us. In this chapter, we have fleshed out for us the four relationships that constitute being created in the image of the Creator: a relationship with the earth, a relationship with others, a relationship with the self, and a relationship with the living God.

As we walk through the story in Genesis 2, we will both rejoice and grieve. As we see what we were created to be, we will all the more grieve over what we have become, and I trust that we will begin to long afresh for the original "right-related-ness" for which the Relationship at the center of the universe called us into being.

RELATIONSHIP WITH THE EARTH

We were created for a relationship with the earth: "Then the LORD God formed man of dust from the ground" (Gen 2:7).[7]

The story emphasizes this relationship by a play on words. The word for "man" is *adam*. The word for "ground" is *adamah*. *Adam* is of the *adamah*. This play on words is also found in Eng-

---

7. For a helpful synopsis of creation care from a biblical perspective, see Richard Bauckham, *The Bible and Ecology: Rediscovering the Community of Creation* (Waco, Tex.: Baylor University Press, 2010).

lish: Human, *Humus*. Humans are of the *humus*. Earthlings are of the earth.

What Genesis 2 tells us is that we are not human apart from our bodies. "Fully human, fully alive" is embodied existence. I do not have a body; I am a body. This means that the problem with humanity is not the body. Of course, our bodies do not work the way they were originally made to work. Something has gone wrong, as we will learn later in Genesis. But we cannot blame our trouble on the body.

We were made for a relationship with the earth. To be human is to be an embodied creature. I emphasize this because over the centuries, there has been a tendency to ignore or even deny the fundamental materiality of our humanity. This has led to two opposite nonhuman lifestyles. One is asceticism, or legalism. This lifestyle says, "Since I am not my body, I will deny its physical needs. I will deny the need for food, sex, and exercise." Yes, there is a place for fasting. Yes, there is a need in a fallen world to take care not to be driven by merely physical needs and drives. But I am my body. I cannot pretend otherwise.

The other nonhuman lifestyle is hedonism, or license. This lifestyle says, "Since I am not my body, I can do whatever I want with it. What I do with my body does not affect the real me. I can fill it with whatever I want, and this will not affect me. I can give into any desire I want, and it will not affect me." We see on TV night after night the demise of body-soul existence, with tragic consequences. As Lewis Smedes says, "nobody can really do what the prostitute and her customer try: nobody can go to bed with someone and leave his soul parked outside."[8] What I do with my

8. Lewis B. Smedes, *Sex for Christians: The Limits and Liberties of Sexual Living* (Grand Rapids: Eerdmans, 1976), 132.

body I do with me. This is how Dietrich Bonhoeffer puts it: "From it [the earth] he has his body. His body belongs to his essential being. Man's body is not his prison, his shell, his exterior, but man himself."[9]

Is not all of this affirmed in the rest of the story, in particular the gospel of Jesus Christ? The Christmas story tells us that God took on a human body; God became a fully embodied creature. As John says, "the word became flesh" (John 1:14). As one of the ancient hymns of the church puts it, "when thou tookest upon thee to deliver man, thou didst not abhor the Virgin's womb."[10] Or as we read in Hebrews 2:14, "since the children share in flesh and blood, He [Jesus] Himself likewise also partook of the same." The Easter story tells us that the incarnate Lord rose bodily. He did not shed bodily existence. Yes, he transformed it, but he rose in a body, ever to live in a body. The second-last chapter of the Bible tells us that our destiny is not just to go up to heaven, to be ghostly beings. Our destiny is to go to "a new heaven and a new earth" (Rev 21:1) More accurately, a new heaven and a new earth will descend to this earth, and we will be restored to a whole and holy bodily existence.

Whatever else we can say about the Christian vision of life, authentic Christian living is always lived in and congruent with the body. All the disciplines of spiritual life involve the body. Prayer,

9. Dietrich Bonhoeffer, *Creation and Fall: A Theological Interpretation of Genesis 13*, rev. the editorial staff of SCM Press (trans. John C. Fletcher; New York: Macmillan, 1959), 46.

10. From "Te Deum Laudamus," as written in *The Book of Common Prayer and Administration of the Sacraments* [. . .], (Toronto: Anglican Book Centre, 1962), 8.

meditation, worship, study, singing, and serving all involve the body.[11] For I do not have a body; I am a body.

RELATIONSHIP WITH OTHERS

We were also created for relationship with other creatures. "It is not good for the man to be alone" (Gen 2:18).

A common refrain in Genesis 1 is that "it was good." We hear it seven times, and then we hear, "It was very good" (v. 31). But here there is something that is not good: "It is not good for the man to be alone." We were made for relationship with other creatures, especially other creatures created in the Creator's image and likeness. This is why it is right to lament loneliness. It is not good for us to be alone, for God is not alone. Humanity in the image of God is co-humanity. So, in one of the most tender speeches God makes in the story, God says, "I will make him a helper suitable for him" (2:18).

God first brings to Adam all kinds of animals. God is not playing games with Adam, for animals do alleviate the aloneness of humans to some degree. In bringing animals to Adam, God is showing us this and is, I think, blessing this fact. Our delight in our pets delights the Creator. When God brings the animals to Adam, Adam begins to give them names. I am reminded of a song Bob Dylan wrote about this entitled "Man Gave Names to All the Animals."[12] In naming the animals, Adam is exercising one of the capacities that reflect the nature and character of God. Adam is

11. Dallas Willard, *The Spirit of the Disciplines: Understanding How God Changes Lives* (1988; paperback ed., New York: HarperCollins, 1991), 18-19.

12. Bob Dylan, "Man Gave Names to All the Animals," *Slow Train Coming*, Columbia MOVLP1459, 1979, LP.

conceptualizing and compartmentalizing; he has begun to order his world. As David Atkinson says, when this happens, "man the scientist is not too far away."[13]

But in the animals, Adam does not find the promised helper. Take careful note of the phrase "suitable for him." The phrase (*b* + *neged*) literally means "according to what is in front of," or "corresponding to," or "equal and adequate to."[14] The helper who will alleviate the aloneness has to be both like the man but different from the man. I like how Karl Barth unpacks the unpleasantness of the phrase. He says that if the helper is only like Adam, loneliness will not be alleviated, because Adam would only see himself. But if the helper is only different, Adam's loneliness would not be alleviated because the helper would not fit with Adam.[15]

So God creates woman. She is the helper suitable for Adam because she is both like him and yet different from him. In the female human, the male human meets someone who is both like him and yet different from him. In the male human, the female human meets someone who is both like her and yet different from her. Take note of the word "helper." "I will make him a helper suitable for him" (v. 18). The word the text is using is *ezer*, which means "one who comes to the aid of someone in need." It comes into play in names like Eliezer, meaning "God is helper." In fact, in the rest of the Bible, the word *ezer* is used mainly of God; God is the great helper. Recognizing this is crucial in understanding the creation of the woman. When *ezer* is used of God, he comes to those who

13. Atkinson, *The Message of Genesis 1-11*, 69.
14. Francis Brown, S. R. Driver, and Charles A. Briggs, *The New Brown-Driver-Briggs-Gesenius Hebrew English Lexicon* (Peabody, Mass.: Hendrickson, 1979), 617.
15. Barth, *Church Dogmatics* 3/2, 290.

are in need. Kenneth Bailey, who has spent his whole adult life studying and teaching the Bible in the Middle East, says that this word "does not refer to a lowly assistant but to a powerful figure who comes to help/save someone who is in trouble."[16] Bailey continues by observing that women "are placed by God in the human scene as the strong who come to help/save the needy (the men)."[17] This is a powerful assertion of female dignity. Male humans simply cannot make it without female humans. History demonstrates this over and over.

The apostle Paul believes this. In 1 Corinthians 11:9 he writes, "For indeed man was not created for the woman's sake, but woman for the man's sake." Woman was not created for man to do whatever he wanted with her, but *because of* man, because man was alone and was not yet able to be fully human. She was created because the man needed an *ezer*, someone strong to help him in his helpless state.

God put Adam to sleep, took one of his ribs, and fashioned the rib into a woman. As Matthew Henry put it in the eighteenth century, woman is "not made out of his (Adam's) head to rule over him, nor out of his feet to be trampled upon by him, but out of his side to be equal with him, under his arm to be protected, and near his heart to be beloved."[18] Take note of how the text mentions both sexes in Genesis 1:26–27: "Let Us make man [humankind] in Our image, according to Our likeness. . . . God created man in His own image, in the image of God He created him; male and female He

16. Kenneth E. Bailey, *Paul Through Mediterranean Eyes: Cultural Studies in 1 Corinthians* (Downers Grove, Ill.: InterVarsity, 2011), 310.

17. Ibid.

18. Matthew Henry, *Commentary on the Whole Bible: Genesis to Revelation*, ed. Leslie F. Church (Grand Rapids: Zondervan, 1961), 7.

created them." Adam is not yet fully human until Eve is created. Male-man is not yet fully human without female-wo-man.

And this is brought out in another play on words. The word for male is *ish*. The word for female is *ishah*. *Ish* is not yet human-in-the-image-of-God until *ishah* is made. Does this mean that we have to be married to be fully human? Right after God presents the woman to the man, the text does speak of marriage: "A man shall leave his father and his mother, and be joined to his wife; and they shall become one flesh" (2:24). But the text is not saying that only the married are humanity in the image of God. It is simply saying that we cannot be fully human unless male and female live in co-humanity. We need one another in our lives. This is what we see in Jesus—a man who was not married but was fully human because he had women in his life.

God brings the woman to Adam, and Adam says, "This is it!" Actually, what he says is "This is now bone of my bones, / And flesh of my flesh; / She shall be called Woman, / Because she was taken out of Man" (v. 23). The words are in poetic form. The first human speech is a love poem! "This is it"—not only "This is the helper," but "This is humanity." Now you have done it, God!

RELATIONSHIP WITH THE SELF

We were created for a relationship with the self: "And the man and his wife were both naked and were not ashamed" (v. 25). Does this mean we were originally created to live in a nudist colony? No. "Naked and not ashamed" is the Middle Eastern way of saying, "I can be myself without masks. I need not create a self to present to others. I can be who I am and not be ashamed." Wow! We were created to be able to look at ourselves—body, mind, heart, and soul—and say, "Oh, what a work of beauty you are!" Can you imagine that? There is no need to cover up, no need to hide. There is no shame.

RELATIONSHIP WITH GOD

This takes us to the fourth relationship: we were created for a relationship with God. Without this relationship, none of the other relationships work. "Then the LORD God formed man of dust from the ground, and breathed into his nostrils the breath of life" (2:7). Until the Creator breathes his breath into us, we are not yet fully human. We are only "candidates" for humanity.[19] We become human when the Creator breathes into us. It is when the Creator gives us mouth-to-mouth that we come to life. It is when the Creator kisses us that we humanoids become living beings.

Two major implications emerge from the picture that Genesis 2 sketches. One is accountability. Since God shapes us, he has the right to determine the rules, to set the agenda. This is the point of the trees, the tree of life and the tree of the knowledge of good and evil, which we will grapple with in the next chapter. God has the authority to tell us how to live the human life, which means it is possible to come to the end of one's life and hear, "You lived by your own agenda and missed the point." The second implication is intimacy. God shapes Adam from the ground. The verb is the same one used when a potter takes a hunk of clay and carefully, tenderly shapes a precious jar. Then God breathes into Adam's nostrils, touching lips to lips. This is such an intimate picture, too intimate for some, telling us that to be human is to share the life of Another.

19. Helmut Thielicke, *How the World Began: Man in the First Chapters of the Bible*, (trans. John W. Doberstein; Philadelphia: Fortress, 1961), 83.

To be human is to be breathed into by Another. To be human is to be indwelt by the life of Another.

This fourfold relationship is what is meant by *shalom*. It is what the Bible means when it uses the words "kingdom of God." And it is why Jesus Christ comes into our world. He is all we were meant to be. He can make all four relationships work again. He is the helper humanity has been waiting for. He makes us "fully human, fully alive." Blessed be his name!

4

Only One Command

Genesis 2:16–18

In Genesis 2 we are given an expansive picture of what and who we were created to be. In pictographic form we see what it means to be created in the image of a relational God: We were created for a fourfold relational harmony. We were created for a relationship with the earth, a relationship with others, a relationship with the self, and a relationship with God.

According to Genesis 2, all this hinges on one command: "The LORD God commanded the man, saying, 'From any tree of the garden you may eat freely'" (v. 16). God has generously provided for human existence and wants humans freely to enjoy it all. "From any tree of the garden you may eat freely; but from the tree of the knowledge of good and evil you shall not eat, for in the day that you eat from it you will surely die" (vv. 16–17). This is the only command that God gives in the Garden of Eden, and I submit to you that it is the only command God has ever given. All other commands are but another way of speaking this one.

Interestingly, this is not the first command God gives in the story of Genesis 1–11. In chapter 1, in the song that sets the stage for the story, God speaks ten creative commands:

"Let there be light" (v. 3).

"Let there be an expanse" (v. 6)

"Let the waters below the heavens be gathered . . . and let the dry land appear" (v. 9).

"Let the earth sprout vegetation" (v. 11)

"Let there be lights in the expanse of the heavens" (v. 14).

"Let the waters teem with swarms of living creatures, and let birds fly above the earth" (v. 20).

"Be fruitful and multiply" (v. 22).

"Let the earth bring forth living creatures after their kind" (v. 24).

"Let us create man [humankind] in Our image, according to Our likeness" (v. 26).

"Be fruitful and multiply, and fill the earth . . . and rule . . ." (v. 28).

We have here ten creative commands, the original Ten Commandments!

This helps us then appreciate the commandments God spoke to Moses on Mt. Sinai thousands of years after the creation. It turns out that God speaks those Ten Commandments (Exod 20:1–17) to make it possible for us to live in the fullness and freedom of the Ten Commandments of creation. If we could keep the Ten Commandments from Mt. Sinai, we would live in the blessing of the Ten Commandments spoken "in the beginning," especially if we lived the first commandment, "You shall have no other gods before me" (Exod 20:3).

We return now to the Garden, to the first relational commandment, the only commandment God gives in the Garden: "From any tree of the garden you may eat freely; but from the tree of the knowledge of good and evil you shall not eat."

THE TREE OF LIFE

Before we grapple with the one command, I want to take a moment to examine the tree of life, which stands in the middle of the Garden. It is mentioned in 2:9, but it does not have a significant role in the story until verses 22–24, when God decides to block the path that leads to it. Why, one might ask, is there so little said about the tree of life and so much attention given to the tree of the knowledge of good and evil? I think Dietrich Bonhoeffer gives the best answer. In his book *Creation and Fall*, he writes,

> It was in the middle—that is all that is said about it. The life that comes forth from God is in the middle. This means that God, who gives life, is in the middle. In the middle of the world which is at Adam's disposal and over which he has been given dominion is not Adam himself but the tree of divine life. Adam's life comes from the middle which is not Adam himself but God. It constantly revolves around this middle without ever making the attempt to make this middle of existence its own possession. It is characteristic of man that his life is a constant circling around its middle, but that it never takes possession of it. And this life from the middle, which only God possesses, is undisturbed as long as man does not allow himself to be flung out of his groove. Adam is not tempted to touch the tree of life, to lay violent hands on the divine tree in the middle; there is no need at all to forbid this; he would not understand the prohibition. He has life.[1]

What Adam does not have is the knowledge of good and evil, hence the reason for the one command in the garden: "From any tree of the garden you may eat freely; but from the tree of the

---

1. Dietrich Bonhoeffer, *Creation and Fall*, 51.

knowledge of good and evil you shall not eat." Again, there is only one command.

CLARIFICATIONS

In order to be clear about what God is after in this command, we need to make a number of clarifications.

First, prohibiting us from eating from the tree of the knowledge of good and evil (we must always say the full name) is in no way unfair or unreasonable. God has given humanity all we need to live "fully human, fully alive." Here in the beginning we have everything we need. In his "do not eat," God is not prohibiting something we need. We do not need to eat from the tree of the knowledge of good and evil. God is not being unfair or unreasonable.

Another clarification is in order: as the Creator, the Lord God has the right to make the rules, even if they are unfair or unreasonable. The Creator of the game has the right to determine how the game is played. One of the scariest things I have ever heard anyone say is "No one is going to tell me how to live my life." It is truly frightening when "no one" includes the Creator. The Creator has the right to make the rules. And there is, at the root, only one rule.

Third, God gives this prohibition for our good. God is warning us, "If you eat from this tree, you will die." Note well that God does not say, "I will punish you," or, "I will make you die," or, "I will kill you." God says, "If you eat from this tree, I will not need to punish you. The natural consequence of eating from this tree is death. Sooner or later you will die."

All of God's commands, including the Ten Commandments and the Sermon on the Mount, are given not to ruin our lives, but to prevent us from ruining our lives. If I were supervising the construction of a tall building and told my workers, "Do not jump off the ledge," would I be seeking to ruin their lives, to stifle their joy

Norman Dodeman
"my boss is always in"

and creativity? No, I would be caring for my workers. I would be telling them about the way the universe works. Apples always fall down. It is the law of gravity. So too with people who step off the ledge! Imagine one day a worker saying, "Well, I think the boss is an old fuddy-duddy. 'In the day you jump you will surely die.' What does he know?" So off the worker jumps, from the thirty-second floor. At first he experiences exhilaration, and he is heard to say as he passes the twenty-second floor, "So far, so good." The ending, of course, is death. In a similar way, God prohibits us from eating from the tree of the knowledge of good and evil for our good, and rejection of his command, while it may seem exhilarating at first, is ultimately disastrous.

Fourth, giving this prohibition reveals God's respect for us human beings. God is treating us as free, rational creatures. Giving such a command to a robot would be nonsensical. As Larry Richards puts it, "there is no moral dimension to the existence of a robot; it can only respond to the program of its maker. . . . To be truly like God, man must have freedom to make moral choices."[2]

Fifth, in giving this one command, God is taking a large risk. God has created a beautiful world, a world that is "very good" (Gen 1:31). It is paradise in every sense of the word. God then places in the world a creature who has the capacity to choose—and who just might make the wrong choice. The great German preacher Helmut Thielicke expresses the risk powerfully. In a sermon he presented at the end of World War II in a bomb-damaged sanctuary in Stuttgart, he explained that when God comes to create human beings,

2. Larry Richards, *Let Day Begin: Studies in Genesis and Job*, Bible Alive Series (Elgin, Ill.: David C. Cook, 1976), 55-56.

one can almost detect something like a hesitation or even a recoil. In any case, it is the kind of bated breath with which we ourselves are familiar when we approach a decisive point in some piece of work on the success of which everything depends. We stop and stand off for a while. It may be the experience of a roofer who has covered a church steeple with shingles and then in one final, risky effort must set the cock upon the peak, or of a dramatist who sets out to compose the main and key scene in his play.

So when God pauses before he composes man into his creation, we sense that there is a risk connected with it: will the creation of man mean the coronation of creation or its crucifixion? Will creation reach its pinnacle when there is added to its creatures a being who rises above the dull level of reflex and instinct, who is endowed with mind and will, and is capable of living as a partner and co-worker of God his Creator? Or is the creation of this being called "man" the first stage in a tremendous descent that starts in the Garden of Eden and leads to a disturbed and desolated earth, that transforms the child and image of God into a robber and a rebel, and through him carries war and rumors of war to the farthest planets?

Coronation or crucifixion of creation—that is the question here. And we understand why God pauses and hesitates, for he is facing a risk. What a breath-taking thought! Is it not almost blasphemous even to think of such a thing?

And this is the way it was. In setting over against himself a being to whom he gave freedom and power he risked the possibilities that the child would become a competitor, that the child would become a megalomaniacal rival of the Creator. . . .

This venture of God in which he bound himself to man—and exposed himself to the possibility of being reviled, despised, denied, and ignored by man—this venture was the first flash of his love. God ventured, as it were, his own self. He declared himself ready to suffer the pain the father endured when he let the prodigal son go into the far county, when he allowed deep wounds to be inflicted upon his heart, and still would not give up his child of sorrows. This line reaches its end in Jesus Christ. There God exposed himself to his rebellious children, put himself at their mercy, and let his most beloved die by their hand but for them.[3]

A sixth clarification is that in God's command we are not confronted with a choice between good and evil. It is one tree, the tree of the knowledge of good and evil. It is not two trees, a tree of good and a tree of evil. God does not create something evil and then place it alongside something good and call us to make a choice. If God had created an evil tree, wrote Francis Schaeffer, "then we would have here a concept like the Hindu idea that eventually both good and evil, cruelty and non-cruelty, spring from God and thus are finally equal."[4]

My final clarification is that the prohibited tree is not called "the tree of knowledge." A great deal of confusion has been caused by carelessly referring to the tree of the knowledge of good and evil as "the tree of knowledge." Even as brilliant a thinker as Erich Fromm read it incorrectly, and he held the view that Genesis is teaching us that God does not want humanity to know, to think, to use our brains.[5] This is a lamentable misunderstanding. God is most certainly not afraid of human beings gaining knowledge. What are we going to discover that could possibly surprise or threaten him? What are we humans going to learn that will send God into a panic? God delights in our discovering truth, in learn-

3. Thielicke, *How the World Began*, 60-61.

4. Francis A. Schaeffer, *Genesis in Space and Time: The Flow of Biblical History* (Downers Grove, Ill.: InterVarsity, 1972), 71.

5. Erich Fromm, *Escape from Freedom* (New York: Farrar & Rinehart, 1941), 34.

ing all about the created order. God finds great joy in our finding out how the universe works, how our bodies and minds and hearts work. God wants us to know as much as we can about his handi-work. I delight in the knowledge of so many in my church. I stand in awe of the carpenters and bakers and geologists and financial analysts and chemistry teachers and psychologists and mothers of little children. God made us to learn and know information, and God wants us to use our brains. It is a false spirituality that asks us to stop thinking in order to believe. The prohibited tree is not the tree of knowledge; it is the tree of the knowledge of good and evil.

THE KNOWLEDGE OF GOOD AND EVIL

The phrase "the knowledge of good and evil" refers to a partic-ular kind of knowledge, and when we trace how the idiom is used in the rest of the Bible, we understand why God prohibits it. It turns out that only God has the knowledge of good and evil—only God can have it and live. In Scripture the idiom is used in refer-ence to human beings, specifically children and the elderly. Chil-dren are said not to have it: "Moreover, your little ones . . . who this day have no knowledge of good and evil" (Deut 1:39; see also Isa 7:15). Children, of course, have knowledge. When we have our lit-tle grandchildren with us for a week, we find out they know a great deal. They know good, and they know evil. But they do not have "the knowledge of good and evil." Elderly people, according to the Bible, have lost this knowledge: "I am now eighty years old. Can I distinguish between good and bad [Can I know good and evil]?" (2 Sam 19:35). Oh, eighty-year-olds have knowledge, knowledge that needs to be shared. They know good, and they know evil. But what eighty- and ninety-year-olds are beginning to lose is "the knowledge of good and evil." So what is this idiom all about? Children do not have it, the elderly have lost it, and those in between think they have it.

Daniel P. Fuller, the first biblical theologian under whom I had the privilege to study, has done the most complete work on the phrase. After working with every use of the idiom in the Bible, Fuller wrote, "It would appear that to the original readers of Genesis 2, the expression 'to know good and evil' signified the possession of that maturity which frees one from being dependent on someone else for guidance on how to act wisely."[6] This is what little children do not have, and what we lose as we age. "To know good and evil" signified the capacity to live independently, without anyone else's help in making one's way through life. Fuller concludes,

> The command not to eat of the tree of the knowledge of good and evil would then mean that Adam and Eve were not to aspire to that maturity possessed only by God, whereby they might consider themselves to be independent of him and able enjoy a fulfilled life by taking matters into their own hands and making their own decisions for their future welfare.[7]

Only God has that kind of knowledge. Only God can live independently of another.

6. Daniel P. Fuller, "The Unity of the Bible" (unpublished lecture notes for "Hermeneutics," taught at Fuller Theology Seminary, winter semester 1970), VIII 1-2, p. 3. Fuller subsequently explained further implications of this insight in *The Unity of the Bible: Unfolding God's Plan for Humanity* (Grand Rapids: Zondervan, 1992), 177-184.
7. Ibid., 182.

ONLY ONE COMMAND

This is how I paraphrase the only command God gave in the Garden:

> Adam, you are what you are because of me, your Creator. You are a glorious creature, magnificent beyond what you yourself know. I have made you to be dependent on me for life. All I ask of you is that you be you—a creature, a human being. You are free. But do not use your freedom to try to be other than you are, a dependent creature. Do not try to be your own god. For all your magnificence, you cannot be your own god. You be you, and I will be me. Do not try to be what I am. I tell you this for your own sake. If you try to be me, if you try to be an independent being, you will ruin your world. You will die.

There is tremendous love in that command. God wants us truly to live. He is warning us that should we sign a declaration of independence from God, we would be signing our death certificate. He gives only one command, and it is this: "Do not try to live apart from me; do not try to live without me." It is the one command that he is speaking to every human every moment of every day. "Do not aspire for the knowledge that makes you think you can live without me. Stay dependent on me."

But Adam did not believe God. Adam and Eve thought they could make it on their own. They took the fruit and ate it (Gen 3:6), and in so doing they "cast off all dependence on God" and took upon themselves the responsibility of making life work.[8] When they did this, they discovered that they were not able to make it all work. Eating the fruit of the tree of the knowledge of good and evil

8. Ibid., 183.

did not give them the knowledge of good and evil, nor did it make them independent. Instead, Adam and Eve had become dependent on drives and forces beneath their dignity. They discovered that they were not God and that instead of becoming more like God, they had become less like the humans God made them to be.[9]

But the Creator did not give up. God went after Adam and Eve, and God comes after us. God comes all the way down into the garden that has become a cemetery and calls us back to the original intent. Jesus, the one true human, calls out to us, "Truly I say to you, unless you are converted and become like children, you will not enter the kingdom of heaven" (Matt 18:3). Why become a child? Because they are unable to make life work on their own. Jesus then says to us, "I am the true vine" (John 15:5), referring, perhaps, to the tree of life. "I am the vine, you are the branches; he who abides in Me and I in him, he bears much fruit, for apart from Me you can do nothing."

There is only one command here. All other commands are variations on the same theme. "Trust me," God is saying. "I will be God; you be human. I will be the Creator; you be the creature. Live in intimate dependence on me."

---

9. James D. G. Dunn, *Christology in the Making: A New Testament Inquiry into the Origins of the Doctrine of the Incarnation* (Philadelphia: Westminster, 1980), 101.

5

Messing with Our Minds

Genesis 3:1–7

"Did God say . . . ?" (Gen 3:1, NRSV).

This is an apparently innocent question posed by an apparently benign being. It carries the sense of "Would a good God ever say anything like that? If God really is for you, if God really wants your very best, would he ever say, 'You shall not'?"

No part of the story makes better sense of our story than what we read in Genesis 3:1–7. Here we have revealed for us the fundamental struggle of human existence. Here we learn what we never would have discovered on our own: someone is messing with our minds. An enemy is messing with our minds with regards to the one command God has given humanity.

REVIEW

Let us review what we have learned in previous chapters.

From Genesis 1, we discovered what every person alive today needs to hear: The universe is not an accident. It did not just "pop" into being out of nothing; Someone wanted it to come to being.

We also discovered that we humans are not an accident either; Someone wanted us to come into being. The living God made us happen.

We learned as well that we humans were made in the image and likeness of God. Nothing else in all of creation bears this significance. "Let us make man [humankind] in Our image, according to Our likeness" (v. 26). We were brought into being to represent the Creator in and to the rest of creation and to reflect the nature and character of the Creator. When the rest of creation looks at us, it is to see something of who the Creator is and what the Creator is like. What dignity!

From Genesis 2 we discovered what being made in the image of God involves. The living God is a relational God. Indeed, the living God *is* relationship. To be made in the image of the relational God is to be made for relationship. In this chapter of Genesis, we see the fourfold relational existence for which the relational God has made us: a relationship with the earth, a relationship with others, a relationship with the self, and a relationship with the living God. "In the beginning" all four relationships worked, and they worked in harmony.

In our study of Genesis 2, we also learned that the enjoyment of that fourfold relational harmony hinges on only one command. After giving the first humans everything they needed to live "fully human, fully alive," God told them, "From any tree of the garden you may eat freely; but from the tree of the knowledge of good and evil you shall not eat, for in the day that you eat from it you will surely die" (vv. 16–17).We discovered that the phrase "knowing good and evil" has a particular meaning. We discovered that to For the first readers of Genesis, "the knowledge of good and evil" would have been understood to refer to the kind of knowledge that makes us think we can live independently of anyone else.[1] We do not need this kind of knowledge. Indeed, such knowledge is the kiss of death.

Then, in Genesis 3, the serpent enters with his apparently innocent question, "Did God say . . . ?"

THE SERPENT

Who or what is this serpent? From the rest of the Bible, we learn that the serpent is an enemy of God. The serpent does not like the living God. We are not told why. All we are told is that he experiences the living God as a threat and opposes all that God desires.

From the rest of the Bible, we learn that the serpent in the Garden is the being called Satan or "the devil." The word "Satan" simply means "adversary" or "accuser," especially an adversary or accuser of God. The word "devil" means "slanderer" or "deceiver," especially someone who slanders or speaks deceptively of God. Jesus later calls this being not only a "liar" but "the father of lies" (John 8:44; see also 2 Cor 11:3; Rev 12:9; 20:2).

Why does the author of Genesis 3 not call the serpent "Satan" or "the devil"? Perhaps Genesis 3 does not want to give humanity an excuse for disobedience and the resulting fall. Genesis wants to keep clear who is responsible for the ruin of God's good world. The devil does not bring about the collapse of the fourfold relational harmony. Yes, he enters the picture and starts corrupting Adam and Eve's minds, but he does not cause the collapse of our fourfold relational existence. We do. We sometimes hear, "The devil made me do it," but that is never true. The devil can entice us to sin, but

---

1. Fuller, *The Unity of the Bible*, 182.

in every case of sin, we are the ones who make ourselves do it. Genesis 3 does not use the terms "Satan" or the "devil" to make sure he does not get the credit he seeks. The author simply calls him "the serpent."

It is important to take note that Satan is a mere creature, a "beast of the field which the Lord God had made" (Gen 3:1). He was not, however, created as the devil, as we shall see below; rather, he was created as a good creature but at some point made a choice that resulted in him becoming evil (Isa 14:13–14). That Satan is a created being is good news, because this means that he can also be de-created. This is what the Garden text wants us to realize. The being who chose to become God's enemy was made by God and therefore can be un-made by God.

It was C. S. Lewis who put things into perspective for me. He wrote a book entitled *The Screwtape Letters*, in which he imagines a senior devil helping a junior devil do the work of undermining and undoing the faith of a new Christian. In an introduction he wrote for a reissue of the book, he says,

> The commonest question is whether I really "believe in the Devil." Now, if by "the Devil" you mean a power opposite to God and, like God, self-existent from all eternity, the answer is certainly No. There is no uncreated being except God. God has no opposite. No being could attain a "perfect badness" opposite to the perfect goodness of God; for when you have taken away every kind of good thing (intelligence, will, memory, energy, and existence itself) there would be none of him left.
>
> The proper question is whether I believe in devils. I do. That is to say, I believe in angels, and I believe that some of these, by the abuse of their free will, have become enemies to God and, as a corollary, to us. These we may call devils. They do not differ in nature from good angels, but their nature is depraved. Devil is the

opposite of angel only as Bad Man is the opposite of Good Man. Satan, the leader or dictator of devils, is the opposite, not of God, but of Michael [the archangel].[2]

God has no opposite! The serpent was created by God, but not to be serpentine. The snake was made by God, but not to be snaky. God did not create the devil as the devil. God created an angel, a good angel, who exercised freedom in a wrong direction and became evil. Now that he is evil, this creature does not like the living God or what the living God makes.

In corrupting Adam and Eve's mind, this serpent uses an effective three-step process. It is to this process that we now turn.

STEP ONE: ISOLATION

In the first step the serpent isolates the woman from the man, from human community. He knows that by ourselves we are sitting ducks. No human being can stand alone. To be more to the point, none of us can keep believing alone. We need community in order to keep believing. We need fellowship in order to be strong in faith.

One of the movements of our time is a shift toward what some are calling "a church-less faith." The church is not all it ought to be, and because in some cases the church is so problematic, it is argued by some that one simply ought to leave the church and develop a faith that is entirely independent from church.

2. C. S. Lewis, *The Screwtape Letters* and *Screwtape Proposes a Toast* (New York: Macmillan, 1961), vii.

In 2010 Christian author Anne Rice announced that she was quitting the church, "in the name of Christ," as she put it.[3] She had become famous for writing books about a vampire, and after coming to faith in Jesus in 1998, she had written two fabulous books on Jesus: *Christ the Lord: Out of Egypt*, which is about his early childhood,[4] and *Christ the Lord: The Road to Cana*, which is about his early ministry.[5] But by 2010 she had had it with the church. She explained that she had not given up on Jesus, just on the church.

I understand and share some of her concerns. But I grieve for her, for very few people can stay faithful to Jesus on their own. As problematic as Christian community can be and has always been, we need each other to keep believing.

The serpent gets Eve by herself, isolated.

STEP TWO: QUESTIONING

The serpent then gets her to question God's word. He does not come as a devil with a pitchfork, but rather comes as an interested fellow seeker: "Did God say . . . ?" (v. 1, NRSV). This approach is, of course, much more effective than coming with a pitchfork, for it allows him to flatter Eve by suggesting that she can think about reality as well as, or even better than, God.

Here I quote Helmut Thielicke once again. He writes, "The first thing that strikes us is this: The drama of temptation, which now begins and puts a sudden end to the vision of a sound and healthy

---

3. "Reason for Quitting Christianity," Anne Rice: The Official Site, accessed September 12, 2017, at <http://www.annerice.com/Chamber-Christianity.html.>

4. Anne Rice, *Christ the Lord: Out of Egypt* (New York: Knopf, 2005).

5. Anne Rice, *Christ the Lord: The Road to Cana* (New York: Knopf, 2008).

world, begins not with the crash of the kettle drum but rather with the sound of oboes. One might even say that it has in it hymn-like motifs."[6] He continues,

> The overture of this dialogue is thoroughly pious, and the serpent introduces himself as a completely serious and religious beast. He does not say: "I am an atheistic monster and now I am going to take your paradise, your innocence and loyalty, and turn it all upside down." Instead he says: "Children, today we're going to talk about religion, we're going to discuss the ultimate things."
>
> Well, something like that immediately inspires confidence. After all, blackguards and rascals do not dabble in such topics. When you talk about pious things you immediately secure for yourself the alibi of serious-mindedness and sincerity.
>
> So he begins by asking, "Did God—this God whom we all revere; even I, the serpent, honor him dearly—did our revered God say that you should not eat of any tree of the garden?"
>
> In other words, the serpent is trying to start a discussion, something like a theological discussion about the "Word of God." So there is not a trace of doubt—oh, no! The devil himself believes in God. He takes his stand on the fact of "God."
>
> In any case, he seems always to plan his tactics from this quarter. The Tempter in the wilderness too did not say to Jesus Christ: "You are a fool to obey your heavenly Father." He too cited nothing but Scripture passages and pious sayings when he urged Him to make bread of stones, leap from the pinnacle of the temple, and accept the kingdoms of this world from his, the devil's hand. The devil acts more pious than a nun and knows his Bible better than a professor of the Old Testament or a Jehovah's Witness. This reptile would even lift his eyes devoutly to heaven, if he had the eyelids to do it with.

6. Thielicke, *How the World Began*, 123-124.

So this is the first point that we must note here: the Tempter always operates in disguise. He hides behind a mask of harmless, indeed, pious benevolence. All temptations in life begin in sugared form.[7]

STEP THREE: TWISTING

In the insidious second step, the serpent twists God's word. He does it ever so slightly at the beginning, and he does it blatantly by the end of the seemingly pious conversation. The key to understanding this story is that God's enemy twists God's words in a specific direction, wanting us to make a false deduction about God's nature and character. Listen to the serpent's first speech: "Indeed, has God said, 'You shall not eat from any tree of the garden'?" (3:1). Look at what the serpent has done. He leaves out the word "freely." God said, "From any tree of the garden you may eat freely" (2:16). The serpent also transfers the prohibition "you shall not" from "the tree of the knowledge of good and evil" to "any tree of the garden." Here he is twisting God's words.

Satan would try this same tactic with Jesus. He would quote God's word to Jesus, twisting it ever so slightly. But it would not work, for Jesus would know God's word better than the enemy. Today, the evil one still approaches us with God's word but uses it out of context or altered in some small way.

Later in the conversation the serpent employs a different tactic. He makes a suggestion as to the real reason God prohibited them from eating from the tree of the knowledge of good and evil, saying, "God knows that in the day you eat from it your eyes will be opened, and you will be like God, knowing good and evil" (v. 5).

7. Ibid., 124-125.

What he is doing here is raising suspicion about the goodness of God. He is proposing the idea that God might be holding back on something. He is getting Eve to wonder about God's motives. To paraphrase what the serpent is saying here, "Eve, God is speaking his 'you shall not' because he really does not want the best for you." The serpent is raising the possibility that God is stingy. Of course, he is wrong. Did God say, "You shall not eat from any tree in the garden?" No, God did not say this. God said, "From any tree of the garden you may eat freely" (2:16). He only prohibited them from eating from the tree of the knowledge of good and evil. God only prohibited us from trying to live independently of him, which is a good prohibition.

The serpent also uses this tactic with all of God's commands. He sneaks in the suspicion that God speaks prohibitions—"you shall not"—because God really does not want the best for us. Bonhoeffer explains that "the serpent pretends somehow to know something about the profundity of the true God. . . . The serpent claims to know more about God than man. . . . The serpent knows of a greater, nobler God who does not need such a prohibition."[8]

EVE'S RESPONSE

Now listen carefully to Eve's response. Something has gone wrong in her soul. "From the fruit of the trees of the garden we may eat; but from the fruit of the tree which is in the middle of the garden, God has said, 'You shall not eat from it or touch it, or you will die'" (3:2–3). Notice how she misquotes God's words, revealing the fact that she is now suspicious of God. She leaves out "any" and "freely." God said, "From any tree . . . you may eat freely."

---

8. Bonhoeffer, *Creation and Fall*, 66.

Eve leaves out those words of generosity, saying, "From the fruit of the trees we may eat." Eve also makes slight additions to what God said. She identifies the tree from which they are not to eat as the tree "in the middle of the garden." The prohibited tree, the tree of the knowledge of good and evil, is not in the middle; the tree of life is in the middle (2:9). This addition suggests that the prohibition is becoming a problem for Eve. She also says that she and Adam were not to eat the fruit "or touch it" (3:3). God never said "Do not touch." That might be implicit in God's prohibition against eating from it, but God never said it. Again, Eve seems to be starting to doubt that God is wholly disposed toward humanity's good.

Notice also that she plays down the severity of the warning. "Or you will die," she says. God had said, "You will *surely* die" (2:17). The slight changing of God's words signifies that Eve is now beginning to question God's character. I detect that the serpent is leading her to think, "Would a good God really let us die? Would a good God really make a statement like 'You will surely die'?"

A final observation is that Eve does not speak of God as God speaks of God. The text of Genesis 2–3 speaks of God as "the LORD God," not just the generic "God." "The LORD" in Hebrew is *Yahweh*, the name God uses for himself, the name he wants to be called. "Yahweh" is God's personal name, his covenant name: "I will take you for My people, and I will be your God" (Exod 6:7); "All I am is placed at your disposal; all that makes me God I give to you." Having left out "any" and "freely," having added "in the middle" and "do not touch," her suspicion is now truly revealed in leaving out "the LORD." God is now only "God"—not Yahweh God, the good and generous God who makes himself wholly available to humanity.

THE TRUE AGENDA

In his response to Eve, the serpent abandons subtlety and reveals his true agenda. "You surely will not die! For God knows that in the day you eat from it your eyes will be opened, and you will be like God, knowing good and evil" (Gen 3:4–5). The serpent calls God a liar, telling Eve that she "surely will not die." To paraphrase, the serpent is saying here, "Why would a good God ever say you humans will suffer the consequences of disobedience? What is the big deal about one little act? How could such a little act possibly ruin anything, let alone lead to death? How silly, Eve! You surely will not die."

According to the serpent, God's lie stems from the motive of not wanting humans to be like him. To paraphrase further, the serpent says, "Eve, God does not want you to be like him; he does not want you to be as happy as he is. That is why he has spoken this prohibition."

It is interesting that the serpent states that Eve can become like God. He is not entirely wrong here. Choosing to eat of the tree of the knowledge of good and evil does lead to independence and, in that sense, becoming like God, the independent and intra-dependent one.[9] But we humans cannot live independently; only God can. We can never be like God in that way. We cannot live as our own gods and live.

The serpent's twisting of God's words twists Eve's thinking. She concludes that God is withholding something she and Adam need. So, as the text tells us, she "took from its fruit and ate; and she gave also to her husband and he ate" (v. 6). And they began to die.

---

9. As made clear in the rest of the Bible, God is triune.

HOW DOES THIS STORY MAKE SENSE OF OUR STORIES?

So, how does this part of the story make sense of our stories?

First, it reveals the nature of temptation. We are not initially tempted to do something overtly evil. We are tempted to doubt the goodness of God. And then, doubting God's goodness, we are tempted to take charge of our own wellbeing and become the captains of our own destinies.

Imagine being out on a lake, waterskiing. The tempter comes up alongside us disguised as a waterski coach: tanned, muscular, the words "no fear" printed on his swim trunks. "Hey, how's it going?" he says. "Do you like the boat driver? He says you have to hang on to the rope. Ever asked why? You do not see him hanging onto a rope, do you? Are you sure you can trust him? Nice enough guy. But can you trust him? Like, does he really care that you get the best ride possible? The first time he sees you really enjoying yourself, he will dump you. Besides, I am here to tell you that you do not need the rope. In fact, you do not need the boat!"

Silly! But no more silly than what the serpent tempts us to think. "God says, 'Lose your life for me and the gospel.' Right. See, I told you he does not want your best. 'If you want to really live, be servant of all.' Like, what is this noise? I am telling you, he does not want you to enjoy life like he does."

The story also reveals the nature of sin. Sin is not just disobedience. Sin is not just rebellion. Sin is not just ungodly deeds. At its root, sin is unbelief. Sin is not believing that God is as good as he says he is. Every particular sin is but the fruit of the prior sin of unbelief.

Why do we steal? Because we no longer believe God can or will take care of us, so we think we have to take matters into our

69

own hands. Why do we lie? Because we no longer trust God to take care of us, so we take matters into our own hands.

Every act of sin is therefore an insult to the character of God: "Sorry God, but this time you cannot be trusted, so I will have to be god right now."

Through this part of the story, we also discover the nature of our nature once we decide God cannot be trusted. In choosing to live independently of God, we do not become independent creatures; we become dependent—on the self. The nature of our nature apart from God is egocentricity. The self is placed at the center, and the self becomes the master and the source of wisdom and strength. Of course, our fallen nature is also expressed in evil thoughts and deeds, but it is chiefly expressed in self-preoccupation. This is a terrible captivity, and I hate it when I see it in myself.

We sinned into existence a creature that was never intended to exist: a creature centered on itself. This is the source of all our misery. This is cause of war and injustice and poverty and ecological destruction. "I, me, mine, myself" is the creed of humanity apart from God. It is the driving force of so much of our existence— driving us into a deep mine from which we cannot free ourselves.

When the self is at the center, we are not free. We become prisoners to a god who cannot bear the weight of our worship. From this bondage we need a Savior, someone who in sacrificial love lays his self aside, who empties himself of all his rightful privileges and descends into the depths to bring us up into the freedom of selfless love.

CAN I TRUST THE CREATOR?

This brings us to the most important way this part of the story makes sense of our stories. It poses the most critical decision of our lives: can I trust the Creator? It confronts us with the question who is right, the Creator or the serpent. Is the Creator for me or not? So much of life around us makes it hard to trust. I know. In a fallen world so much seems to call into question the character of the Creator, and the serpent uses it all to corrupt our minds, to encourage us to conclude that the Creator cannot be trusted. "See! I told you. You are having a hard time because he is not really for you. He does not want you to be alive and free."

The critical decisions every day are:

> Can I trust the One who made me?
> Will I trust the One who made me?

This is why the rest of the story leads us to the feet of Jesus Christ. In Jesus we see who the Creator is. In Jesus we see that the serpent is lying. In Jesus we see that God is for us. "He who did not spare His own Son, but delivered Him over for us all, how will He not also with Him freely gives us all things?" (Rom 8:32). There is that word again: freely!

"Did God say . . .?" Eve should have said, as we need to say again and again,

> Yes, God did say, 'You shall not,' but not about the trees of the gar-
> den. Of any tree of the garden we may freely eat. But if we eat from
> the tree of the knowledge of good and evil, the tree that makes us
> think we can live independently of God, we shall die. For we were
> created as dependent creatures, and in that trust I choose to live. I
> refuse your lie. In Jesus' name, be gone!

That's what she should have said.

6

Grace Outruns the Avalanche

Genesis 3:8–24

Genesis 3:8–24 has to be one of the saddest stories ever told. Many people tell me that after reading the text they feel profoundly sad. And rightly so, for in this story we are reading about the collapsing of God's good world.

The living God had, out of love and great joy, brought humanity into being in paradise. The living God had, with deep affection and much delight, formed us to live in relationship with the earth, with others, with the self, and with God. And in Genesis 3 the fourfold relational harmony is falling apart, quickly unraveling. To put it more bluntly, the relational harmony is dying.

I think what makes the story so sad is that we are seeing it played out in our time right before our very eyes in terribly sad ways. The news headlines confirm that the Genesis text is speaking truth, sad truth.

GRACE IN GENESIS 3

But sad as the sad story is, the fact that the story is told is a grace. We should be thankful that the God who sings the joyful story of Genesis 1 and tells the happy story of Genesis 2 also bothers to tell the sad story of Genesis 3. This is because the story is telling us what every person alive today implicitly feels. The story is telling us that things are not now the way they are supposed to be. The text is describing death, and the text is telling us that death is not supposed to be present. Just knowing this fact brings some relief and comfort.

G. K. Chesterton, a witty philosopher-theologian of the early twentieth century, puts it best. At one point in his life, he was wrestling with the phrase "the best of all possible worlds," a phrase coined by the German philosopher Gottfried Leibniz.[1] Leibniz and others argued that since the Creator is good, and since the Creator is all-powerful, he must have chosen this world for us as the best of all possible worlds. Chesterton wrestled with this because he felt, as most humans have felt, that this can't be the best of all possible worlds. In his book *Orthodoxy* he writes, "The modern philosopher had told me again and again that I was in the right place, and I had still felt depressed even in acquiescence. But I had heard that I was in the wrong place, and my soul sang for joy, like a bird in spring."[2]

He describes how he had previously heard

---

1. Gottfried W. Leibniz, *Theodicy* (trans. E. M. Huggard; Don Mills, Ont.: J. M. Dent & Sons, 1966). This book was first published as *Essais de theodicee sur la bonte de Dieu, la liberte de l'homme et l'origine du mal* in 1710.

2. G. K. Chesterton, *Orthodoxy* (Vancouver, B.C.: Regent College Publishing, 2004), 94.

that good was not merely a tool to be used, but a relic to be guarded, like the goods from [Robinson] Crusoe's ship—even that had been the wild whisper of something originally wise, for, according to Christianity, we were indeed the survivors of a wreck, the crew of a golden ship that had gone down before the beginning of the world.[3]

Then Chesterton says,

But the important matter was this, that it entirely reversed the reason for optimism. And the instant the reversal was made, it felt like the abrupt ease when a bone is put back in the socket. I had often called myself an optimist, to avoid the too evident blasphemy of pessimism. But all the optimism of the age had been false and disheartening for this reason, that it had always been trying to prove that we fit in to the world. The Christian optimism is based on the fact that we do not fit in to the world [as it is].[4]

As a side note, this is why we cannot base our ethics on the way things are. Things are not the way they are supposed to be, so we cannot simply make our ethical choices based on what we see around us.

Remarkably, while this story is sad, it is full of grace for the survivors of the shipwreck. The text describes what Gerhard von Rad called "the avalanche of sin," the quickly moving disintegration of the four relationships for which we were originally made.[5]

3. Ibid., 93.
4. Ibid.
5. Gerhard von Rad, *Genesis: A Commentary* (trans. John H. Marks; Philadelphia: Westminster, 1961), 148-150; Gerhard von Rad, *Old Testament Theology*, Vol. 2, *The Theology of Israel's Prophetic Traditions*, (trans. D. M. G. Stalker; New York: Harper & Row, 1962), 163-164.

But as the text painfully describes the avalanche of sin, it also describes the quickly moving grace of God. Indeed, the text is telling us that grace is outrunning the avalanche of sin. The Garden may have become a cemetery, but in the cemetery there are amazing signs of life because of God's amazing grace.

So let us go through the story two times. The first time, let us take seriously the way the text describes the avalanche of sin. The second time, let us also take seriously the way the text describes grace outrunning the avalanche.

In our last chapter we saw how the enemy of God, the serpent, the embodiment of evil, came into the picture and started corrupting the first humans' minds, as he tries to do with all their offspring. He twists God's good command in ways that raise suspicion about the goodness and generosity of God.

Sadly, the first humans buy into the serpent's twisting, and they conclude that they must have the knowledge of good and evil. They go out on their own in an attempt to make life on earth work according to their own plans and desires. They decide that they do not need to remain in a dependent relationship with the Creator.

The result is what we read in Genesis 3. All four relationships unravel.

RELATIONSHIP WITH GOD UNRAVELLED

Our relationship with God unravels. What was previously a relationship of trust, delight, love, and intimacy is now marked by suspicion, doubt, fear, and guilt.

"And the man and his wife hid themselves from the presence of the LORD God among the trees of the garden" (Gen 3:8). They hide themselves—so terribly sad! God has not even spoken to Adam and Eve. They simply hear, as the text puts it, "the sound of the LORD God walking in the garden in the cool of the day," a sound they have heard many times before, a sound that filled their hearts with joy. "The Lord is drawing near!" But now, having disobeyed the one good command, having moved out of the proper posture of a creature dependent on the Creator, the sound of the living God walking in the garden makes them afraid, and they feel ashamed and try to hide.

The same is true of all of Adam and Eve's offspring. We all try to hide. Of course, there is a sense in which we all seek God, for the deepest recesses of our being long for the Creator and Sustainer of our lives. But sadly, as J. Barrie Shepherd says, "the characteristic human pose is one of hiding."[6] We sense the gentle stirring of God's movement in our lives, and we hide.

We try to hide under noise. We keep the radio and television on. We keep the iPod plugged into our ears. Yes, sometimes we do this for good reasons, but often we do it as an unconscious attempt to silence the sounds of God walking in the places where we live and work.

We try to hide in our busyness. Yes, often we are active because we really care about others or because we are alive with creative ideas and energy. But often we stay busy so we do not have to deal with the sound of the Creator moving around us.

We hide through chemicals. We use alcohol or drugs to drown out the sound of the Wholly Other.

We hide behind skepticism. There certainly are real intellectual challenges involved in trusting God, and I do not want to minimize them. But often, rather than not believing because of a true lack of evidence, we use these challenges as excuses not to believe

---

6. J. Barrie, *Encounters: Poetic Meditations on the Old Testament* (New York: Pilgrim, 1983), 71.

because our hearts know that believing means changing and we do not want to change.

We hide by not accepting responsibility for our choices. In Genesis 3, when God does speak and confronts the first humans about their disobedience, they shift the blame. Adam blames Eve. Eve blames the serpent. Adam even blames God: "the woman whom You gave to be with me, she gave me from the tree" (Gen 3:12).

The most sophisticated hiding place of all is religion. It is very subtle. We tend to think that humans design religions as part of our search for the one true living God. That is true to a certain degree, but for the most part it is not quite right. The apostle Paul, commenting, I think, on Genesis 3, says in his letter to the Romans,

> For even though they knew God, they did not honor Him as God or give thanks, but they became futile in their speculations, and their foolish heart was darkened. Professing to be wise, they became fools, and exchanged the glory of the incorruptible God for an image. . . . For they exchanged the truth of God for a lie, and worshiped and served the creature rather than the Creator. (Rom 1:21–23, 25)

Because the one true living God is now experienced as a threat, we invent a god with whom we can comfortably live. We shape a god in our image, one who does not upset our lives. We create a god we can handle, who baptizes our own understanding of reality. One church historian even suggests that some churches pay their pastors to protect them from the true God![7]

---

7. Richard F. Lovelace, *Dynamics of Spiritual Life: An Evangelical Theology of Renewal* (Downers Grove, Ill.: InterVarsity, 1979), 84.

What was originally a relationship of trust, delight, love, and intimacy is now marked by suspicion, doubt, fear, guilt, and hiding.

RELATIONSHIP WITH THE SELF UNRAVELLED

This wounded relationship with God affects the relationship with the self. When we no longer know the Creator as he is, we no longer know ourselves as we are. Thus, the relationship with the self also begins to unravel. The separation from God is now carried into the personality as a separation from the self.[8] Originally we were "naked and were not ashamed" (Gen 2:25), integrated and at peace with ourselves. Now it is "I heard the sound of You in the garden, and I was afraid because I was naked" (3:10). "Who told you that you were naked?" (v. 11), God asks in great sadness.

Since a wounded relationship with God caused this wounded relationship with the self, only a healed relationship with God can heal the relationship with the self. Psychologists can, to a certain degree, help people understand themselves. But healing will finally come only when humans move out of the place they were never intended to occupy and become creatures before the Creator once again.

RELATIONSHIP WITH OTHERS UNRAVELLED

This alienation from God, resulting in alienation from the self, has immediate effects for the relationship with others. Adam blames Eve, and God's good gift of a life partner begins to unravel. Instead of accepting responsibility for his own actions and con-

---

8. Schaeffer, *Genesis in Space and Time*, 98-99.

fessing his own guilt, Adam projects it onto Eve. All their subsequent offspring follow this pattern. We blame parents, culture, and the environment—and they do have a role to play!—but ultimately, we choose to talk, feel, and act the way we do.

Alienation from God and from the self results in the breakdown of human community. The relationship between the man and the woman was originally one of trust, care, attentiveness, servanthood, and mutuality. Now it is marked by competition and the desire to dominate. God says to Eve, "Your desire will be for your husband, and he will rule over you" (v. 16). The verbs "desire" and "rule" will be used in Genesis 4, where God will say to Cain, the firstborn of Adam and Eve, "Sin is crouching at the door; and its desire is for you, but you must master [rule] it" (v. 7).

The relationship between the man and the woman—"I will make him a helper suitable for him" (2:18)—becomes one in which each seeks to dominate the other. Genesis 3:16 is not the way it is supposed to be. God is not prescribing a relationship of dominance; he is sadly describing what happens when we disobey the one command.

RELATIONSHIP WITH THE EARTH UNRAVELLED

Then Genesis 3 tells us that all the spiritual, psychological, and relational alienation that comes as a result of sin also affects one's relationship with the earth; it too unravels. The avalanche gathers up the created order in its sweep.

The ground is cursed (v. 3:17), and there is pain in childbirth (v. 16). Adam now struggles with thorns and thistles as he tills the ground. Eve now endures agony and pain as she brings children to the world. God has said, "Be fruitful and multiply" (1:28), but now creation groans to be fruitful, and creatures groan to multiply.

GRACE IN RELATIONSHIPS WITH THE EARTH, OTHERS, AND THE SELF

But God "keeps pace with this avalanche."[9]

Although the earth no longer works as freely and fruitfully as God designed it to work, it still yields food—an abundance of food. This is a result of God's grace. Every garden that grows in the cemetery is a sign of grace. Every farm yielding produce in our fallen world is a sign of grace. This is why it is so appropriate that every time we eat, we "say grace." God did not have to keep the creative properties of the earth going. God could have left the earth to die completely. But thanks to him, the earth still yields food.

Although the relationship between the man and the woman has been damaged, they still want each other; they still care. Every time any relationship works, it is a sign of grace. Every time two people get along, it is a sign of grace. Every time a man or woman chooses the way of servanthood, it is a sign of grace. Why does the world, even the unbelieving world, honor people like Mother Teresa or Nelson Mandela? They are signs of grace: rejecting the way of dominance and lordship and choosing the way of submission and servanthood.

Notice what the text says when Adam calls his wife "Eve": "Now the man called his wife's name Eve, because she was the mother of all the living" (v. 20). The name "Eve" means "living." Although the relationship is unraveling, Adam still delights in Eve, and he recognizes that although death has entered the world, God still brings forth life. A doctor once told me, "The birth of every baby is a sign that God has not given up on the world."

9. Von Rad, *Genesis*, 148-150; von Rad, *Old Testament Theology*, 2:163-164.

Grace keeps pace with the avalanche of sin.

Although the relationship with the self is now problematic, God meets the humans in their shame, making coverings for their nakedness. What a tender scene! "The Lord God made garments of skin for Adam and his wife, and clothed them" (v. 21). Earlier in Genesis 3, the first humans tried to cover their shame by making clothes out of fig leaves (v. 7). Here God does better. As Walter Brueggemann puts it, "God does (3:21) for the couple what they cannot do for themselves (3:7). They cannot deal with their shame. But God can, will, and does."[10]

GRACE IN THE RELATIONSHIP WITH GOD

And then the relationship with God. Full of grace!

God asks the question "Where are you?" (v. 9). The point here is that God still wants the relationship. The question is pure grace. Obviously he knows where they are—and where we are. God asks the question to draw us back into fellowship. Because we are afraid and feel such shame, God draws, rather than drives, us out of hiding.[11]

God could have said, "Adam and Eve, I see you under that bush. Now come out, and let us talk." But those words would have driven them further into hiding. Adam would have whispered to Eve, "Shhh! Be very still. Maybe he will go away." Or God could have said, "Adam and Eve, come out. I will not hurt you. I still love you." But they would not have believed the words. Guilt drowns out the grace notes in God's voice. So God asks a question. Ques-

10. Brueggemann, *Genesis*, 50.
11. Derek Kidner, *Genesis: An Introduction and Commentary*, Tyndale Old Testament Commentary Series (Downers Grove, Ill.: Tyndale, 1967), 70.

tions have a way of getting past our defenses. It is harder to remain still before a question. "Where are you?" A tremendous grace! A sign that God wants to reestablish the relationship of trust and intimacy.

As we have already noted, God then clothes the fearful, ashamed humans. He does not pull them out of hiding and make them stand before him in shame. He does not yank the fig leaves off them, making them endure his all-searching gaze. No, "the LORD God made garments of skin . . . and clothed them" (v. 21). God knows our felt need to hide, so he provides a hiding place in his presence!

"Where are you?" The question calls us out of the darkness into the light. And in the light he covers us! He covers our shame. The prophet Isaiah would later declare, "I will rejoice greatly in the LORD, / My soul will exult in my God; / For He has clothed me with garments of salvation, / He has wrapped me with a robe of righteousness" (Isa 61:10).

God's act in the garden-become-cemetery prefigures the gospel of Jesus Christ. For where did God get the skins to cover the first humans? From a dead animal. A death takes place in order to cover their shame and take away their fear. Blood was shed to make God's hiding place for ashamed sinners. Looking at the cross and quoting from the Psalms, the apostle Paul declares, "Blessed are those whose lawless deeds have been forgiven, / And whose sins have been covered" (Rom 4:7).

Even after this there is more grace. God guards the way to the tree of life (v. 24), which is an enormously merciful grace because it protects Adam and Eve from horrible judgment. God does not want them to go on living in independence, in a fallen state. This is not the best of all possible worlds, and God does not want us to grab hold of the tree of life and go on living forever in this not-best-of-all-possible-worlds. God does not want humans to live forever in alienation from him, from ourselves, from others, and from the earth, so he guards the way to the tree of life. Grace is outrunning the avalanche!

THE PROTO-GOSPEL

In the garden-become-cemetery, the Creator makes a great promise that the church has for centuries called the "proto-gospel." Speaking to the serpent who is rightfully "cursed," God says, "I will put enmity / Between you and the woman, / And between your seed and her seed; / He shall bruise you on the head, / And you shall bruise him on the heel" (v. 15). "He [the seed of the woman] shall bruise you [the serpent] on the head, / And you [the serpent] shall bruise him [the seed of the woman] on the heel."

It is in this promise that we most see grace outrunning the avalanche of sin. God is promising that one day, a child of the woman will come and do battle with the serpent. The child will represent the whole human race, and he will come and deal a deathblow to the serpent. The serpent will try to hurt him ("bruise his heel"), but in hurting the seed of the woman, he would be overcome ("bruise you on the head").

This promise and its fulfillment is what holds the rest of the Bible together. This promise is the thread weaving the rest of the story into the story of grace. From that day on, from the day God made the promise, the question will be "Who is this seed? Who is this seed of the woman who crushes the head of evil?"

The implication of the promise is that this seed will come and restore the fourfold relational harmony for which we were created. This seed, this child, this boy, this man, this Adam will free us from the power of death and bring us back into relational wholeness.

The longing for the seed is, for me, most passionately expressed by the prophet Isaiah:

> The people who walk in darkness will see a great light . . .
> For you shall break the yoke of their burden. . . .
> For a child will be born to us, a son will be given to us;
> and the government will rest on His shoulders.
> And His name will be called Wonderful, Counselor, Mighty God,
> Eternal Father, Prince of Peace.
> There will be no end to the increase of His government or of [His]
> peace. (9:2, 4, 6–7)

Then he came, the seed of the woman: "But when the fullness of time came, God sent forth His Son, born of a woman" (Gal 4:4)! Right from the beginning of his life on this fallen earth, he faces the rage of the serpent. The serpent tries to crush him while just a baby through King Herod. The serpent tries to crush him while an adult through the religious authorities and through the political authorities. On the cross, the serpent thinks he has finally crushed him, only to discover—to his horror—that he himself has been crushed by the seed of the woman!

This is what Mel Gibson was trying to convey in his movie *The Passion of the Christ.*[12] If you have seen the movie, you will remember the snaky, serpentine figure coming in and out of the story, and you will remember that at the very moment Jesus dies, there is a loud scream, and we see the serpent spiraling down into the abyss, screeching in agony. For in the moment the serpent bruised the seed of the woman on the heel, the seed of the woman bruised the serpent on the head.

12. *The Passion of the Christ*, directed by Mel Gibson (Santa Monica: Icon Productions, 2004).

Do you remember what else happens in the moment Jesus dies? The Gospel writers love to tell it! In the moment Jesus dies, the curtain in the Temple—the curtain that guards the way into the Holy of Holies, where the Holy Ones chooses to dwell—is torn in two from top to bottom. On that curtain were embroidered cherubim, angelic beings God posted in the garden to guard the way to the tree of life. At the moment the seed of the woman dies, the curtain with the cherubim is torn into two, announcing that the way is now open. For Jesus Christ is humanity as we were supposed to be. He is humanity living in utter, complete dependence on his Father. In him it is safe to eat from the tree of life. Indeed, he is the tree of life.

On Easter morning Jesus stands in a garden-become-cemetery. Mary Magdalene does not completely recognize him; she thinks he is the gardener. And she is right! He is not the cemetery gardener on duty that day, but the Gardener. God the Gardener walks again in the garden, calling Mary, and us, to himself.

Grace is outrunning the avalanche of sin!

E. Stanley Jones, a missionary to India, observes that "the early Christians did not say in dismay: 'Look what the world has come to'"—which is what we say during our first reading of Genesis 3—"but in delight, 'Look what has come to the world!'"—which is what we say during our second reading of Genesis 3. "They saw not merely the ruin, but the resources for the reconstruction of that ruin. They saw not merely that sin did abound, but that grace did much more abound."[13]

<hr>

13. E. Stanley Jones, *Abundant Living* (Nashville: Abingdon, 1942), 183, quoted in James Montgomery Boice, *Philippians: An Expositional Commentary* (Grand Rapids: Zondervan, 1971), 104-105.

Jones could say that because that is what the apostle Paul trumpeted through the collapsing Roman Empire. "But where sin increased, grace abounded all the more," literally "grace super-abounded" (Rom 5:20). And the next verse: "so that, as sin reigned in death, even so grace might reign to eternal life through Jesus Christ our Lord."

Grace will always outrun sin.

7

Grace Outside the Garden

Genesis 4

Like the previous chapter, Genesis 4 is a sad story. In fact, it is more than sad. It is a dark story. The avalanche of sin is speeding up, rushing into ever deeper darkness. The avalanche is heading into death, literally so. The first child born to the first humans murders his brother.

But as is the case with Genesis 3, so it is with Genesis 4. Although a very sad story, Genesis 3 is full of grace. And although it is a sad, dark story, Genesis 4 is also full of grace, full of light.

Genesis 3 shows us grace in the garden; Genesis 4 reveals grace outside the garden. Over Genesis 3 we can speak the New Testament claim "Where sin increased, grace abounded all the more [super-abounded]" (Rom 5:20); over Genesis 4 we can speak the New Testament claim "The Light shines in the darkness, and the darkness did not comprehend it" (John 1:5)—or, as the NIV renders it, "the darkness has not overcome it."

Notice that the story is bracketed by miracles. The sad, dark chapter begins and ends with the conception and birth of a child. "Now the man had relations with his wife Eve, and she conceived and gave birth to Cain" (v. 1). "Adam had relations with his wife again; and she gave birth to a son, and named him Seth" (v. 25). In a world falling apart, in a world coming under the power of death, God graces the first human couple with children. As any couple that has struggled with infertility knows, conception and birth are always a miracle. Outside the garden, God is extending amazing grace.

What is said at the birth of each child opens up the meaning of Genesis 4. Of Cain, Eve says, "I have gotten a manchild with the help of the LORD." Of Seth, Eve says, "God has appointed me another offspring [literally "seed"] in place of Abel, for Cain killed him." God has given Eve children.

The sad and dark story of Genesis 4 is full of grace and light— as are all sad, dark stories in which the God of grace and light chooses to intervene.

There is so much in this chapter that helps us make sense of our own stories. Where should we focus?

GRACE FOR CAIN

We could focus on the totally unexpected grace given to Cain the murderer. After God confronts the first person born to human parents for murdering the second person born to human parents, and after spelling out the judgment ("Now you are cursed from the ground," v. 11), Cain cries out, "My punishment is too great to bear!" (v. 13). Your punishment is too great? No punishment is too great for what you did! You lured an innocent man out into the field, and you killed him. Your punishment is too great to bear? You have been banished from the ground that sustains human life. You took life, and now you are reaping the consequences. You are cut off from what sustains life.

But God's response is totally unexpected: "So the LORD said to him, 'Therefore whoever kills Cain, vengeance will be taken on him sevenfold.' And the LORD appointed a sign for Cain, so that no one finding him would slay him" (v. 15). God protects the killer from those who would want to kill him.

Yes, Cain has to leave the ground and carve out an existence "east of Eden," in the desert, "the land of Nod" (v. 16). "Nod" means "wandering." But Cain gets grace, unexpected, unmerited, scandalous grace. God protects the murderer from other murderers. We are not told what "the sign for Cain" is. Is it a protective tattoo that says "Hands off, or you answer to God"?[1] We are not told. All we know is that somehow God will protect Cain the killer from other Cains who want to kill him. Incomprehensibly, God bestows grace on Cain.

The tragedy of the story is that Cain's family will forget about this scandalous grace. By the seventh generation, revenge will be the name of the game. Lamech, Cain's great-great-great-great-great grandson will boast in killing other human beings. Lamech says to his two wives, "Adah and Zillah, / Listen to my voice, / You wives of Lamech, / Give heed to my speech, / For I have killed a man for wounding me; / And a boy for striking me; / If Cain is avenged sevenfold, / then Lamech seventy-sevenfold" (vv. 23–24). A boy merely wounds Lamech, and Lamech kills him. Lamech is not even satisfied with eye for eye, tooth for tooth; he wants life for eye, life for tooth. And even that was not enough! Lamech wants seventy-sevenfold compensation.

Where else in the larger biblical story do we hear those numbers again, seven and seventy-seven? We hear them when Jesus comes to stop the avalanche. The disciple Peter asks, "How often

1. Waltke and Fredricks, *Genesis*, 99.

shall my brother sin against me and I forgive him? Up to seven times?" (Matt 18:21). Peter thinks he is being magnanimous. Jesus replies, "I do not say to you, up to seven times, but up to seventy times seven" (v. 22).

GRACE FOR THE CITY

We could focus on what Genesis 4 reveals about human cities. Cain is driven from the ground, and in verse 14 he says he will be hidden "from the face of God." This is not true, for he will never escape the face of God. He will only *think* that God does not see him. But Cain, driven from the ground and driven from the face of God, builds a city, and he names the city that he builds after his firstborn, Enoch. He builds a city for protection and to sustain human life outside the Garden. Cain moves out of the posture of creature before the Creator and builds a city. Cain has left the true center of life, the living God, and now he puts himself at the center and builds a city. The first human city is built without any orientation toward the Creator. It is built to facilitate life in total independence from the Creator.

Is that not the genesis of most human cities? Are not most built without any reference to God? Are not most built to facilitate life that is independent from God? New York City was founded by people escaping religious influence. There were no churches or synagogues in New York for the first fifteen years of its existence. It followed the lead of the first city: designed for life without God.

Yet there is grace! In Genesis 4, there is grace for the city. God enables the "godless" humans to make their city work. As David Atkinson notes, "civilization begins to grow outside the Garden. Even in the land of restlessness, there is culture, there is art. Surprisingly, it is through Cain the homeless, the fugitive, the prodigal, that God's commission to his people to work and to subdue creation begins to be established."[2] The text speaks of those who "play the lyre and pipe" (v. 21) and those who forge "all implements of bronze and iron" (v. 22). This is grace. That any city works is a sign of grace. Even when the city does not want God, God still gives grace to make it work. God gives creative genius to fallen humanity.

However, the sad fact is, as Derek Kidner observes, that "the family of Lamech could handle its environment but not itself."[3] We will pick up the theme of "God and the city" when we get to Genesis 11 and the story of the Tower of Babel, and we will see how the story points to another grace: God is building a city that will out-dazzle all the cities of the world.

CONTENDING FOR CAIN'S SOUL

The most significant way Genesis 4 helps us make sense of our stories is in the way God relates to Cain. In the opening scene of the story, we find God contending for Cain's soul, as he does for our souls. It is on this grace that I invite you to focus with me.

The two brothers bring their offerings to God. The text says, "The Lord had regard for Abel and his offering; but for Cain and his offering, He had no regard. So Cain became very angry and his countenance fell" (vv. 4–5). Why did Cain become angry? We can understand why this would make Cain sad, and we can understand why it would make him jealous. But angry, so much that it affects his body ("his countenance fell")? Why is he so angry?

Well, at whom is he angry? At Abel? Partly. But mostly, Cain is angry at God. God's regard for Abel and his offering and God's

2. Atkinson, *The Message of Genesis 1-11*, 113.
3. Kidner, *Genesis*, 78.

disregard for Cain and his offering made him "very angry" at God. Why?

WHY WAS GOD PLEASED WITH ABEL?

In order to answer this question, we have to ask another: Why was God pleased with Abel and his offering but not with Cain and his?

Throughout the centuries, the people of God have searched for some basis for God's different responses to the two brothers. So, for example, Philo, an ancient philosopher from Alexandria, Egypt, argued that "Abel's offering was living, Cain's was life-less."[4] Jewish historian Josephus argued that "Cain brought the fruits of the cultivated ground and of trees, while Abel brought milk and the firstlings of his flocks. This latter offering gave the greater pleasure to God, who is honored by those things which grow spontaneously and in accordance with nature, and not by those things which are forcibly produced by the ingenuity of covetous man."[5] Biblical scholar F. F. Bruce rightly calls that interpretation "far-fetched."[6]

Another school of thought sees the distinction in the fact that Abel's offering involved the shedding of blood. Although not espousing this view, William Barclay writes,

> The only offering which a man can bring to God is the offering of the most precious thing that life supplies. Now the most precious

4. Philo, *The Sacrifices of Abel and Cain* 88, quoted in English translation in F. F. Bruce, *The Epistle to the Hebrews* (Grand Rapids: Eerdmans, 1964), 284.

5. Josephus, *Antiquities* 1.54, quoted in English translation in Bruce, *Epistle to the Hebrews*, 284.

6. Bruce, *Epistle to the Hebrews*, 284.

thing that life supplies is life itself; and to the Hebrews blood always stood for life. . . . If that principle be accepted, then the only true sacrifice to God, in those primitive days, was a sacrifice of blood, because blood is life, the most precious thing. Abel's sacrifice was a sacrifice of a living creature; Cain's was not; and therefore Abel's was the more acceptable.[7]

In evaluating this view we need to note that nowhere in the story is it suggested that the brothers were presenting sin offerings. Both brothers simply bring offerings suitable for their vocations.[8] Cain was a tiller of the ground, so he brings what a tiller can offer. Abel was a shepherd, so he brings what a shepherd can offer. Cain brings the fruit of the ground, Abel the best of his flock. Then what is the basis of God's regard for Abel and his offering and disregard for Cain and his offering? The text seems to point to something in Cain's attitude that was not pleasing to the Lord. Note how the author puts it: "The LORD had regard for Abel and for his offering; but for Cain and for his offering he had no regard" (vv. 4–5). The emphasis is on the *person* before the gift. The issue is not the gift itself, but the person presenting the gift. There was something about Abel that pleased God and something about Cain that displeased God. What is it?

The writer of the New Testament letter we call Hebrews says, "By faith Abel offered to God a better sacrifice than Cain" (11:4). Abel's offering was not inherently better than Cain's, but Abel's attitude and orientation were. Abel offers his gift by faith. Abel offers his gift acknowledging that God is God, God is master, God has first place in all things.

7. William Barclay, *The Letter to the Hebrews* (Edinburgh: Saint Andrew, 1955), 148-149.

8. Bruce, *The Epistle to the Hebrews*, 283.

CAIN'S ATTITUDE

So what is Cain's attitude? Martin Luther points out that "Cain could properly and truthfully take pride in his very high nobility, for he was the first to be born of men."[9] Luther suggests that it is possible that Eve, Cain's mother, fostered this pride of first place.[10] When Cain is born, Eve seems to brag: "I have gotten a manchild with the help of the LORD" (Gen 4:1). The words can also be translated "I have gotten a man as the LORD." It is almost as if she is saying, "As the Lord creates, so I have created. As the Lord created Adam, so I have created a man, an Adam."

"I have gotten a man." Eve does not say a "child," but a "man," an Adam, like the Adam the Lord has made. It is even possible that Eve's words can be translated as "I have gotten a man, the LORD." Does Eve then regularly remind her son of his status? "Cain, my son, my man, my Adam, you are the first human being to come from the womb of a woman!" The name Cain likely means "I have gotten" or "gotten one." The name Abel is related to the word that means "no toughness, frailty." It is used in the book of Ecclesiastes: "Vanity of vanities! All is vanity" (1:1)

Thus, from day one Cain thinks of himself as first and as occupying first place. And apparently he comes to expect others to think of him as first. Cain even expects God to think of him as first.

Therefore, as Luther suggests, when Cain offers his gift to God, he is "puffed up."[11] Cain expects God to treat him specially be-

---

9. Martin Luther, *Luther's Works*, Vol. 1, *Lectures on Genesis Chapters 1-5*, ed. Jaroslav Pelikan (trans. Gerorge V. Schick; Saint Louis: Concordia, 1958), 256.

10. This does not mean that she is to blame for the fall.

11. Luther, *Luther's Works*, 1:258.

cause of his firstborn status. "Of course God will have regard for me. I am Cain, the first." He comes before God not by faith, but by works, appealing to something in himself, to his human status. Abel, however, has no such status. He comes before God realizing he has no distinction to claim, nothing by which to obligate God. He comes depending solely on God's mercy and grace—he comes by faith.

You can see, then, that Cain's problem is that he has a faulty view of himself. Just as Cain assumed he had first place with Adam and Eve, so Cain assumes he has first place with God. And what makes Cain so angry is that God does not operate on Cain's system of values. God does not honor Cain's view of himself. Cain is the firstborn. So what? It makes no difference to God, as we see in the rest of Genesis. Faith is what God responds to. In the moment that God does not show regard for Cain and his offering, Cain's self-centered world is threatened. Indeed, it is leveled. And he becomes very angry. God is not playing by Cain's rules.

What makes matters worse for Cain is that God does not accept Cain's view of Abel either. All his life Cain has expected Abel, the second-born, to play by the firstborn's rules. Cain has come to see himself as the center of the universe and therefore sees Abel as one of the orbiting planets. Cain looks at Abel as either someone useful for his own wellbeing or as someone who is an obstacle to his wellbeing. God's regard for Abel changes the playing field.

The fact is, Cain has never really seen Abel as a brother. He calls Abel "brother," but in his heart, Abel has never been on the same level, never an equal. For Cain truly to embrace Abel as a brother, Cain would have to move out of the center.

In our fallen state, we want to be the center of our worlds— and of everyone else's worlds. As long as we keep living with that faulty view of ourselves, no one around us is a brother or a sister.

They are either a means to an end or obstacles in the way. Or worse yet, we do not even notice them.

But God. God does not want Cain to suffer from his faulty view of himself, so in grace God appeals to him to do well: "If you do well, will not your countenance be lifted up?" (v. 7).

"Sin is crouching at the door" (v. 7). God's warning is grace. God portrays sin as a violent animal, ready to pounce on its victim.[12] "Go for it," says sin. "Be the center. Be number one. You deserve the very best." Cain's sin is crouching at the door: "its desire is for you" (v. 7). To paraphrase, God says, "Do well, Cain. Think straight. You are not the center. You do not have first place. The Creator is the center. You and Abel are equals on the circumference.

But Cain will not give up his infantile self-perception, and as a result he "envies God's pleasure in his brother"[13] and becomes angry with God. God warned him, as he warns us, "Deal with your faulty view of yourself, or your faulty view of yourself will consume you."

God was contending for Cain's soul, and God contends for our souls. God, in grace, exposes the Cain in us. God helps us see that when we think we are the center, brothers and sisters around us are reduced to objects to be used, discarded, or neglected.

WHERE IS YOUR BROTHER?

Genesis 4 especially wants us to see that how we view ourselves and others is a symptom of how we view God. Most of the conflict in our world, be it between individuals or nations, is root-

12. Greidanus, *Preaching Christ from Genesis*, 94.
13. Von Rad, *Genesis*, 101.

ed in the Cain-like bent in us all. This is the reason for the gracious question "Where is your brother?" (v. 9). In Genesis 3 grace came through "Where are you?" (v. 9). Now, in Genesis 4, it comes through "Where is your brother?" "Where is your sister?"

"Where is your brother?" is God's call to realize that we are not the center of our worlds. "Me first" is the language of the nursery. "I," "me," "mine," "myself" are the pronouns of Cain, who is stuck in infancy. Jesus comes into our world and calls us into adulthood. "You, Jesus, you are first" is the language of maturity, the language of the soul set free.

God's question "Where is your brother?" is also God's call to see the person next to us as "from the hand of God."[14] Abel came from Eve's womb, but ultimately he came from God. It was God who made Abel happen. It was God who put Abel in Cain's life. But because Cain did not see God at the center, he did not see Abel as a gift. God's question reminds us that people are in our lives because God put them there. We can overlook them, we can hurry past them, we can use them, or, as Helmut Thielicke expresses it, we can "run straight into the arms of God," who gives them as gifts.[15]

This question is also God's call to realize that the Invisible One, the Wholly Other, chooses to meet us in the brother or sister. That is why God cries out to Cain, "What have you done?" (v. 10). Thielicke writes, "Cain not only laid violent hands upon a human being who was a burden to him and whom he regarded as an intruder; he also violated the property of God himself."[16] That is why God takes up the cry of Abel's blood, and that is why God protects Cain from further violence. To disregard the brother or sister—even the

14. Thielicke, *How the World Began*, 197.
15. Ibid., 201.
16. Ibid., 212.

"nobody" brother or sister—is to disregard the God who created them, the God in whom they "live and move and have [their] being" (Acts 17:28).

Is this not what Jesus tells us in his parable of the sheep and the goats?

> But when the Son of Man comes in His glory, and all the angels with Him, then He will sit on His glorious throne. And all the nations will be gathered before Him; and He will separate them from one another, as the shepherd separates the sheep from the goats; and He will put the sheep on His right and the goats on the left.
>
> Then the King will say to those on His right, "Come, you who are blessed of My Father, inherit the kingdom prepared for you from the foundation of the world. For I was hungry, and you gave Me something to eat; I was thirsty, and you gave Me something to drink; I was a stranger, and you invited Me in; naked, and you clothed Me; I was sick and you visited Me; I was in prison, and you came to Me." Then the righteous will answer Him, "Lord, when did we see You hungry, and feed You, or thirsty, and give You something to drink? And when did we see You a stranger, and invite You in, or naked, and clothe You? When did we see You sick, or in prison, and come to You?" The King will answer and say to them, "Truly I say to you, to the extent that you did it to one of these brothers of Mine, even the least of them, you did it to Me." (Matt 25:31–40)

Jesus identifies with all the Abels of the world, all the "nothings." He is telling us what he wanted Cain to understand: we meet him in the Abels—in the powerless, in the "nobodies." If we see ourselves as Cain did, as having the right to first place, we will not see Jesus in those he calls "brothers and sisters."

In his famous sermon entitled "The Weight of Glory," C. S. Lewis articulates this mystery: "Next to the Blessed Sacrament itself, your neighbor is the holiest object presented to your senses. If he is your Christian neighbor, he is holy in almost the same way, for in him also Christ *vere latitat*—the glorifier and the glorified, Glory Himself is truly hidden."[17] I think you can see that God's question "Where is your brother?" is another way for God to ask, "Where am I? Where do you think I am? What you do with your brother or sister you do with me."

Sadly, Cain did not overcome the sin crouching at the door. He could not give up his infantile view of himself. He built a city around his infantile view, and it all culminated in Lamech's infantile celebration of revenge in the city.

But God. God does a new work of grace outside the Garden. He works in Eve's body, causing her to conceive again, and he works in Eve's soul, resulting in a change in her speech. When Cain was born the speech was "I have gotten a manchild" (4:1). But when Seth is born, the speech is "God has appointed me another offspring." Light has broken into the darkness. The mother of all living regains perspective and throws herself on the promise God made in the Garden that one day a seed of the woman would come and crush the serpent. Clearly, and sadly, Cain is not that seed, but God has not given up. He starts over. Seth is born. The promise keeps going.

And miracle of miracles! "Then men [humans] began to call upon the name of the LORD" (v. 26). Outside the garden, in the heart of the city, people "began to call on the name of the LORD."

---

17. C. S. Lewis, *The Weight of Glory* (San Francisco: HarperCollins, 1976), 46.

Keeping His Word

Genesis 5

Although I believe every part of Scripture to be the living Word of the living God, I have to confess that when I am reading the Bible and come to a genealogy, I am tempted to skip it so that I can get to the "good stuff." In more duty-bound moments, I might at least speed read the genealogy. But surprisingly, when we understand what the biblical genealogies are doing, we find that texts like Genesis 5 are indeed "good stuff."

If you have read widely in the Bible, you know that this is not the only genealogy inspired by the Spirit of God. We find a number of them in Genesis 1–11: in chapters 4, 10, and 11. We also find a number in the rest of Genesis: in chapters. 25, 35, 36, and 46. The first nine chapters of 1 Chronicles are one very long genealogy. Matthew begins his Gospel with a genealogy (1:1–17). And Luke follows his telling of Jesus' baptism with a different genealogy (Luke 3:23–28).

THE GENRE OF GENEALOGY

In texts like Genesis 5, we are dealing with a particular literary genre. In the Bible we have poetry, like Genesis 1, the Psalms, and the Song of Solomon. We have what I have been calling pictographs, like the story of Genesis 2–3. We have historical documents, like 1 and 2 Samuel, 1 and 2 Kings, and the book of Acts. We have wisdom sayings, like the text of Proverbs and James. We have prophecy, like Isaiah, Micah, and Amos. We have the Gospels, Matthew, Mark, Luke, and John, which are often said to comprise their own unique literary genre, the gospel genre. We have parables, like those Jesus told to open up the reality of the Word of God. We have epistles, such as Romans, Ephesians, and Philemon. We have apocalyptic, my favorite genre, like Daniel and the most magnificently crafted document in human literature, the Revelation of Jesus Christ. And we have genealogies.

If you read all the genealogies in the Bible, you will discover that each of them is slightly different, not only, of course, because they have different names, but because they are assembled in different ways:

> Some are in the simple form: A gave birth to B, who gave birth to C, who gave birth to D.
> Some are in the form of A gave birth to B, B gave birth to C, C gave birth to D.
> Some periodically add a comment. We see that especially in 1 Chronicles 1–9, which includes comments like "Now Jabez called on the God of Israel, . . . and God granted him what he requested" (1 Chron 4:10) and "Because [Reuben] defiled his father's bed, his birthright was given to the sons of Joseph the son of Israel" (1 Chron 5:1).
> Some simply list the names.

Some "play it forward," beginning with the originator of the line, moving to the son, and to the grandson, and so on: A father of B, B father of C, C father of D. Matthew does this; he begins with Abraham and goes through David to Jesus (Matt 1:1–17).

Some "play it backward," beginning with the last person and tracing back through the line, parent, grandparent, and so on: D son of C, C son of B, B son of A. Luke does this; he begins with Jesus and goes all the way back through David and Abraham, through Noah and Adam, all the way to God (Luke 3:23–38)

Although the genealogies give the names in chronological order, they are not necessarily giving strict chronology. "A son of B" can mean that A is literally the son of B, but it can also mean that A is a descendant of B. Between A and B there can be other literal sons and daughters, grandsons and granddaughters. That is to say, genealogies can skip generations. For example, in Ezra we read of "Azariah, son of Meraioth" (7:3), but in 1 Chron 6:7–10 we learn that there are four generations between Azariah and Meraioth. Matthew says that "Joram [was] the father of Uzziah" (1:8), but in 1 Chronicles we learn that Joram was the father of Ahaziah, who was the father of Joash, who was the father of Amaziah, who was the father of Azariah, who was also known as Uzziah (3:11; see also 2 Kgs 14:21–22, 2 Chron 26:1–2).

Again, all the genealogies give names in chronological order, but the genealogies are not necessarily giving us strict, continuous chronology. This means that we cannot add up all the ages of the persons named in Genesis 5 and work backward to the date of the birth of Adam. James Ussher, a bishop and gifted scholar of the seventeenth century, assumed strict chronology and used Genesis 5 to argue that creation took place on October 23, 4004 BC. That might be true, but it might not. Genealogies cannot give an undisputed answer, for they often skip generations.

THE LESSONS OF GENEALOGIES

The biblical genealogies teach us two things: the nature of history and the value of individuals.

The genealogies teach us that history is linear. History moves. It is not the endless repetition of the same pattern. History is not cyclical. This is the unique contribution of the Judeo-Christian faith to our understanding of time. History moves forward— sometimes downward, sometimes upward, sometimes to the right, sometimes to the left, but always forward. History is heading somewhere. There is a trajectory, a *telos*. This is good news to people caught in religious philosophies of monotonous repetition, and it is good news to people who believe that "history is a conveyor belt of corpses because of Adam's sin."[1] History is linear, not cyclical; we are not stuck in meaninglessness.

The biblical genealogies also teach us that individuals have value. History is not driven by great ideas alone, but by great ideas embodied in individuals who think, make decisions, and act out their ideologies in real time with real people in real communities. The God of history values individuals. Indeed, the genealogies declare that God remembers individuals and names. People matter, and names matter. Our names matter. We count in the unfolding of history.

1. John Piper, "The Fatal Disobedience of Adam and the Triumphant Obedience of Christ," Desiring God, August 26, 2007, at <http://www.desiringgod.org/messages/the-fatal-disobedience-of-adam-and-the-triumphant-obedience-of-christ.> The quotation is from about 17:27.

God's regard for names exacerbates a distress I am currently experiencing: I am having trouble remembering names. I used to be very good at it. I could hear someone's name once or twice and remember it. Now I have to hear it three, four, or five times, and I still might not get it. It matters to me that I cannot remember everyone's name because people matter to me.

God remembers! Indeed, God has a book in which he writes the names of those he claims for himself, the Lamb's book of life, as it is called (Rev 21:27). Your name and my name may never appear in the *Who's Who* of the twenty-first century. No matter. What matters is that they are written in the big book—in God's *Who's Who*.

So, the biblical genealogies help us make sense of our stories by teaching us that history has meaning, that it is linear and not endlessly cyclical. And they remind us that individuals matter.

What does the genealogy of Genesis 5 uniquely teach us? How does this chapter of The Story That Makes Sense of Our Stories make sense of our stories? If I had to give a title to the genealogy of Genesis 5, it would be "Keeping His Word." God, the Creator and Redeemer, the God of justice and mercy, is keeping his word. We see and hear this in four terms the author of the genealogies uses: "begat," "died," "rest," and "took."

BEGAT

First term is "begat." Most modern translations use the longer phrase "became the father of," but the Hebrew uses a single word. "Begat," "begat," "begat." Nine times, "begat." The point is that God is keeping his first creative word. This is why the genealogy begins the way it does: "This is the book of the generations of Adam. In the day when God created man, He made him in the likeness of

God. He created them male and female, and He blessed them and named them Man in the day when they were created" (vv. 1–2).

Where have we heard those words before, "likeness," "male and female," "blessed"? We have heard them in Genesis 1. The genealogy of Genesis 5 is returning to Genesis 1, where God started the flow of history. The genealogy is restating this original creative word. After the sad, dark story in Genesis 4, the story of Cain the murderer and his line deteriorating to the point where Lamech boasts about murdering a boy, Genesis 5 goes back to the beginning and reaffirms God's decision to make a creature in his own likeness. The point is that God is not going to give up. No Cain-to-Lamech family line is going to thwart God's desire to have creatures alive in his image.

"He blessed them" (5:2) echoes the original "God blessed them; and God said to them, 'Be fruitful and multiply'" (1:28). And they did. In spite of human sin, humanity has multiplied and still is multiplying. "Male and female" he created them, with the capacity to be fruitful and multiply. God is going to have his way. "Male and female" alive together, becoming his likeness in the world. Begat.

But not only is God keeping his original creative word, he is also keeping his original redemptive word, the word spoken in the garden-become-cemetery, the word he spoke to the serpent, who had twisted God's good command in the direction of raising suspicion about God's character and intention. God said, "I will put enmity between you and the woman and between your seed and her seed; he shall bruise you on the head, and you shall bruise him on the heel" (3:15). God is keeping his word about bringing into the world the seed of the woman, who will crush the head of evil. In Genesis 4 it became clear that the firstborn human child, Cain, was not the seed. If anything, Cain is dangerously close to being a seed of the serpent. Cain's descendent Lamech clearly had fallen into the serpent's ways. Through this chain of "begats," God will make sure the seed is born.

DIED

The second term in which we see and hear God keeping his word is "died." In the genealogy of Genesis 5, we have the sober refrain "and he died, "and he died," "and he died." Eight times, "and he died." The point is that God is also keeping the original word of judgment. In the only command God gave humanity in the Garden, he said, "You will surely die." "From any tree in the garden you may eat freely; but from the tree of the knowledge of good and evil you shall not eat, for in the day that you eat from it you will surely die" (2:16–17). And they did. And so did all their subsequent offspring. "Died," "died," "died." God is keeping his word. No other text in the Bible puts it as forcefully.

This tells us that God means business. The living God is not like a parent who indulges the child, giving idle threats. God said that "in the day" we declare independence from him, we would not be able to make life work on our own. We would die. And we did. And we still do.

We were not supposed to die. This is the point of the large numbers in the genealogy, the long years people lived. I know it is hard to get our minds around these numbers.

> Adam lived 930 years (v. 3).
> Seth lived 912 years (v. 8).
> Enosh lived 905 years (v. 11).
> Kenan lived 910 years (v. 14).
> Mahalalel lived 895 years (v. 17).
> Jared lived 962 years (v. 20).
> Methuselah lived 969 years (v. 27)!

Lamech lived 777 years (v. 31).
Noah lived 950 years (9:29).

They lived so many years because we were originally created to live a long time—forever in intimacy with God. Again, I know it is hard to imagine. The whole idea raises all kinds of questions. But this is what Genesis 5 brings to the table as we seek to make sense of human existence. We were not supposed to die. Whether the numbers in the genealogy are literal or symbolic or both, the point is that we were not supposed to die.

In Genesis 11, after the flood, the genealogy has smaller numbers, showing that slowly but surely God's word is being actualized.

Shem son of Noah lived 600 years (vv. 10–11).
Arphaxad lived 438 years (vv. 12–13).
Shelah lived 433 years (vv. 14–15).
Eber lived 464 years (vv. 16–17).
Peleg lived 239 years (vv. 18–19).
Reu lived 239 years (vv. 20–21).
Serug lived 230 years (vv. 22–23).
Nahor lived 148 years (vv. 24–25).

"You will surely die." "And he died." Yes, it is depressing, but the genealogy does not want us to live in a make-believe world. The genealogy wants us to face the reality of judgment. Yes, death is not going to have the last word, as we will see in a moment. But death is here and now lives.

Psalm 90 is attributed to Moses. It begins, "Lord, You have been our dwelling place in all generations. / Before the mountains were born / Or You gave birth to the earth and the world, / Even from everlasting to everlasting, You are God" (vv. 1–2). Then verses 3 and 7: "You turn man back into dust / And say, 'Return, O children of men.' . . . For we have been consumed by Your anger / And by Your wrath we have been dismayed." All of humanity is under the righteous wrath of God. We all die, as God said we would.

Jonathan Edwards, a great theologian-pastor of the eighteenth century, regularly contemplated the reality of death. In 1722, at the age of nineteen, while living in New York, he set out a number of resolutions. He read them each week for the rest of his life. These were resolutions that he knew he could only keep by the grace of God.[2] Some of the resolutions were as follows:

> "Resolved, to live with all my might, while I do live" (no. 6).
> "Resolved, never to do anything out of revenge" (no. 14).
> "Resolved, to examine carefully, and constantly, what that one thing in me is, which causes me in the least to doubt of the love of God; and to direct all my forces against it" (no. 25).

I like that one! Another one:

> "Resolved, never to do anything, which I should be afraid to do, if it were the last hour of my life" (no. 7).

One written a year later than the others:

> "I frequently hear persons in old age say how they would live, if they were to live their lives over again: resolved, that I will live just so as I can think I shall wish I had done, supposing I live to old age" (no. 52).

---

2. All of these resolutions are taken from Jonathan Edwards, *The Works of Jonathan Edwards*, Vol. 16, *Letters and Personal Writings*, ed. George S. Claghorn (New Haven, Conn.: Yale University Press, 1998), 753-757.

And this:

> "Resolved, to think much on all occasions, of my own dying, and of the common circumstances which attend death" (no. 9).

Every week, "to think much . . . of my own dying." Is this morbid? No, it is simply facing reality. Edwards knew how fragile life is, and he did not naively live in denial. We all die. When we truly face that fact, we live differently—more simply, more gratefully, more generously.

"And he died," "and he died," "and he died."

It is right to lament the reality of death, because it did not have to be. It is right to cry out in protest. Jesus' weeping at the grave of Lazarus was his "This ought not be."

Genesis 5 is reminding us that death exists, and that "he died" because we humans did not believe God when he told us we could not make it on our own. "He died," "he died," "he died." God is keeping his word.

REST

A third term is "rest." Lamech calls his son "Noah," for "this one will give us rest from our work and from the toil of our hands arising from the ground which the LORD has cursed" (5:29). How Lamech knows this we are not told. The Lamech of the Cain line in Genesis 4 accepts the fact of violence as normal; he even celebrates it. The Lamech of the Seth line in Genesis 5 understands that sin has resulted in a curse and longs to have rest from this curse.

Where have we heard the term "rest" before? We heard it in the Song of Creation, when God establishes the seventh day, the day of rest. Do you see what Lamech sees? God is going to bring us into the blessing of the seventh day. God has something to give us on the seventh day that he has not given in the other six days.[3] God is going to have his way; he is going to bring us into his rest, freed from the curse.

Lamech says that Noah will give us rest, but he is not exactly right. Lamech is illustrating the nature of the prophetic word. He sees the ultimate end, but not how we get there. Prophets always hit the target, but seldom the bull's eye. The target is "rest," but the bull's eye is not Noah. Yes, after the flood, creation is reinvigorated, and the ground more willingly yields fruit. But Noah does not bring the rest, the freedom from the curse. Noah, as righteous a man as he is, is not the seed of the woman. That seed will not come for many generations. But when he comes, he will give us rest. "Come to me," he will say, "all you who are weary and have overburdened yourselves, and I will rest you" (adapted from Matt 11:28).

But Lamech does somehow see, and the genealogy of Genesis 5 preaches, that God keeps his word about the seventh day. God will give us rest from the consequences of human sin.

TOOK

This brings us to the fourth term in Genesis 5 in which we see God keeping his word: "took." The pattern is "he died," "he died," "he died." But the cadence is broken by the startling declaration "Enoch walked with God; and he was not, for God took him" (v. 24).

Amazing! This too is hard to get our minds around. Enoch does not have to go through the process of dying. He is simply

---

3. Wallace, *The Ten Commandments*, 66.

"taken" by God, as the prophet Elijah would be years later (2 Kgs 2:11–12).

Why is Enoch spared the "he died"? Twice the text says, "Enoch walked with God" (vv. 22, 24). This means, I think, that he walked with God in a unique way, in a deeply intimate way, all the time, every day, in every event. He "walked with God." In a world seeking to operate without any reference to God, Enoch walked with God.

God graciously calls all his people to do this. "He has told you, O man, what is good; / And what does the Lord require of you But to do justice, to love kindness, / And to walk humbly with your God?" (Mic 6:8). The apostle Paul will echo the call: "Therefore I, the prisoner of the Lord, implore you to walk in a manner worthy of the calling with which you have been called" (Eph 4:1). "Walk in love" (Eph 5:2). "Walk as children of Light" (Eph 5:8). "Walk by the Spirit, and you will not carry out the desire of the flesh" (Gal 5:16).

Enoch "walked with God," and "God took him." Later Jewish documents would go to elaborate lengths speculating about this. (See, for example, the pseudepigraphal Book of Enoch.) But all the genealogy of Genesis 5 says is that "he was not, for God took him." God chose to spare Enoch the pain of death to show that death will not win in the end. "He died," "he died," "he died," and then, right in the middle of this genealogy, "he was not, for God took him." As Madeleine L'Engle puts it, "already . . . God is trampling on death, telling us that death is not going to have the last word."[4]

God is keeping his word. God created us for fellowship. God created us to enter into life with him, to enter into his own inner life as Father, Son, and Holy Spirit. And God is going to have his

---

4. Madeleine L'Engle, *And It Was Good: Reflections on Beginnings* (Wheaton, Ill.: H. Shaw, 1983), 105.

way. Enoch is Exhibit A. Death will not have the last word over those who seek to walk with the God of life. Eventually the seed of the woman will come. "Begat," "begat," "begat." He will overcome the power of death. But here is the mystery: he will not, like Enoch, be spared death. He will walk right into the jaws of death, and he will let death have its full way with him. And in so doing, he will deal death a deathblow.

Near the end of the Gospel of Matthew, which begins with a genealogy, Matthew tells us that in the moment Jesus dies, "the veil of the temple was torn in two from top to bottom; and the earth shook and the rocks were split. The tombs were opened" (Matt 27:51–52). As he dies, the tombs are opened! In the moment the seed of the woman dies, death loosens its grip and has to let the dead go. Jesus defeats death by dying (Heb 2:14–15). I never tire of repeating what a mentor of mine, Peter Joshua, never tired of repeating: "When death stung Jesus Christ, it stung itself to death."

"And the tombs were opened." As Ravi Zacharias enjoys reminding people, "Jesus did not come into this world to make bad people good. He came into this world to make dead people live."[5] The apostle Paul, who knew the genealogies of Genesis, says, "For since by a man came death, by a man also came the resurrection of the dead. For as in Adam all die, so also in Christ [the New Adam] all will be made alive" (1 Cor 15:21–22). Paul goes on to say what the genealogy of Genesis 5 is pointing toward:

> Behold, I tell you a mystery; we will not all sleep, but we will all be changed, in a moment, in the twinkling of an eye, at the last trumpet; for the trumpet will sound, and the dead will be raised

---

5. Ravi Zacharias, *Cries of The Heart: Bringing God Near When He Feels So Far* (Nashville: Word, 1998), 112.

imperishable, and we will be changed. For this perishable must put on the imperishable, and this mortal must put on immortality. But when this perishable will have put on the imperishable, and this mortal will have put on immortality, then will come about the saying that is written, "Death is swallowed up in victory. O death, where is your victory? O death, where is your sting?" . . . Thanks be to God, who gives us the victory through our Lord Jesus Christ. (1 Cor 15:51–55, 57).

God is keeping his word in the seed of the woman, in the new Adam. God is keeping his word.

9

Starting Over

Genesis 6–9

Ever since I learned the flood story as a little boy, Noah has been for me the model of what it means to walk with God (Gen 6:9). He is out in a desert, far from any lake or sea that could float the ship he built. There is no cloud in the sky, at least none portending a deluge of the magnitude the story describes. He is believing a word spoken by a God he does not see, trusting in a word when nothing in his environment supports it and no one else in his culture believes it.

Rightly does the author of the New Testament book we call Hebrews lift up Noah as a hero of faith (11:7). "Faith is the assurance of things hoped for, the conviction of things not seen" (Heb 11:1). The author of Genesis says, "Thus Noah did; according to all that God had commanded him, so he did" (6:22; see also 7:5). Oh, to have such faith!

OTHER FLOOD STORIES

What has long fascinated me is the fact that this is not the only story of a great flood. Many other cultures in many other places have preserved stories very much like what we have in Genesis 6–9. Francis Schaeffer remarks that "it's interesting that among the common myths in the world's history, no other one is so widespread as the story of the flood."[1] All over the Middle East, throughout China, and among the Native Peoples of the Americas, we find stories of a great flood.

Archaeologists, for instance, have found in the ruins of the ancient Babylonian Empire stories of a flood that follows the same pattern of the story in Genesis 6–9.

> Creation comes into being.
> Humans rebel against the gods in some way.
> A huge flood comes.
> Creation begins anew.

You have likely heard of the *Epic of Gilgamesh*, a Babylonian story told approximately seventeen hundred years before the birth of Jesus by a sage, Ut-Napeshtim, to Gilgamesh, a king on a quest for immortality. According to this story, humanity is becoming too noisy, making it hard for the gods to sleep. One god secretly warns his favorite human to build a boat to save his family. This human does what he is told to do. The flood comes. After the waters recede he offers a sacrifice. Gods crowd "like flies" around the sweet sacrifice and then bestow immortality on the one human.[2]

Early in the twentieth century, many people assumed that what we have in Genesis is a copy or an adaptation of that epic. But few would argue so today, for the simple reason that archae-

---

1. Schaeffer, *Genesis in Space and Time*, 129-130.
2. For more information about the *Epic of Gilgamesh*, see Gordon J. Wenham, *Genesis 1-15*, Word Biblical Commentary 1 (Waco, Tex.: Word, 1987), 159-166.

ologists have found other, different flood stories in other places than ancient Babylonia. Among the ruins of the Sumerian Empire (2,000 BC), for instance, there was a list of kings, divided between "kings before the flood" and "kings after the flood." There is also the *Epic of Atrahasis* from around 1,700 BC in the Semitic Old Babylonian language.[3]

The ancient Near East had not one, but many, flood stories, and although these stories share much in common, Genesis tells a story that is different from the others in some important ways. Compare the *Epic of Gilgamesh* and Genesis:

> In *Gilgamesh*, the gods are offended by the noise humans are making; in Genesis, God grieves over the corruption of sin and the overstepping of boundaries.
>
> In *Gilgamesh*, one human is warned secretly; in Genesis, God warns everyone through the preaching of Noah (2 Peter 2:5).
>
> In *Gilgamesh*, a human pilots the boat; in the narrative of Genesis, Noah has to wait on God.
>
> In *Gilgamesh*, the humans leave the boat at will; in Genesis, Noah leaves at the command of God.

And in Genesis God makes a promise, a covenant that affects the whole universe and all living creatures.

The fact that there are many flood stories reinforces a presupposition from which I work and live, one that I learned while serving in the Philippines from 1985 to 1989. The presupposition is that all cultures, ancient and modern, have myths that are in touch with truth. These myths, though distorting the truth, in some cases grossly so, are rooted in truth. Part of the work of evangelism

---

3. Kenneth Anderson Kitchen, *The Bible in Its World: The Bible and Archaeology Today* (Downers Grove, Ill.: InterVarsity, 1977), 28.

is getting in touch with the truth at the root of these myths and showing how the gospel speaks to it.

The fact that cultures from around the globe have flood stories says to me that something significant really happened, something universal. This is why the apostle Peter can say in his second letter, "By the word of God the heavens existed long ago and the earth was formed out of water and by water, through which the world at that time was destroyed, being flooded with water" (2 Pet 3:4–5). Something happened that was truly cataclysmic. Scientists can tell us that sixty-five million years ago one half to three quarters of all living species disappeared. Why? Something happened, something to which Genesis 6–9 points us.

In this chapter I want to ask three questions about the flood story: "Why did the flood happen?" "What exactly happened in the flood?" and "What does it mean for us now?" This story is referred to by a number of New Testament authors. You might be surprised to learn that Jesus refers to it quite a number of times. How does this part of The Story That Makes Sense of Our Stories make sense of our stories?

WHY DID THE FLOOD HAPPEN?

The flood happened for two reasons. The first is the sin of humanity. We have seen how the author of Genesis 1–11 describes this avalanche of sin and how grace outruns sin. We notice that this avalanche is getting worse and worse—until God chooses to tolerate it no longer.

The first time that we heard the words "the Lord saw" in Genesis 1–11 was in chapter 1, when God finished making his good world. "God saw all that He had made, and behold, it was very good" (v. 31). But as the avalanche continues downward, God sees, and it is not good. "Then the Lord saw that the wickedness of man was great on the earth, and that every intent of the thoughts of his heart was only evil continually" (6:5). The condition of humanity is awful—"every," "only," "continually."

It is texts like these that have led the church to the doctrine of total depravity. I know I am raising something very offensive in our time. The doctrine does not say that we are no good at all. Rather, it says that every part of us has been affected by sin. Our minds, our emotions, and our wills are all affected by sin in one way or another. Again, this is why I say that our ethics can never be built on the way things are. Saying "This is the way I am" proves nothing, because the way I am is not the way I am supposed to be. "What is" is not what is supposed to be, and this is why we need a new heart. "Behold, I was brought forth in iniquity, / And in sin my mother conceived me. . . . Create [*bara*] in me a clean heart, O God" (Ps 51:5, 10).

Take careful note of the word "corrupt" in this Genesis passage: "Now the earth was *corrupt* in the sight of God. . . . God looked on the earth, and behold, it was *corrupt*; for all flesh had *corrupted* their way upon the earth" (6:11–12). This word can also be translated "destroyed," so it could be said that the earth was destroyed before the flood. What God chooses to destroy (v. 13) has already destroyed itself.[4] This is a crucially important truth about the living God: his judgment is him giving humanity the final form of our chosen self-destruction.

The second reason for the flood was the crossing of boundaries. "The sons of God saw that the daughters of men were beautiful [lit. "good"]; and they took wives for themselves" (6:2). "Saw . . . good . . . took." Where have we seen and heard those words before? We have heard them in the story of the fall of humanity: Eve "saw

4. Kidner, *Genesis*, 87.

that the tree was good," and she "took from its fruit and ate" (3:6). The fall took place because humans crossed a boundary, and the avalanche of sin leads to another crossing of a boundary.

The question is "Who are these 'sons of God'?" Some say they are the men of the godly line of Seth described in chapter 5. Some say they are kings or rulers who exert their dominance over women (see Pss 2, 82; 2 Sam 7:14). Some say they are non-human, god-like beings; they are angels who, like the angel who became the devil, rebel against God and his order in the universe. I take that interpretation. In Job we hear of "the sons of God" coming to meet in a heavenly court. One of them is "the Satan," the serpent of old (Job 1:6; Ps 29:1). Jude speaks of angels "abandoning their proper abode" (Jude 6).

Do you see, then, what is going on in the Genesis story? There has been a horrific violation of the created order, a destructive overstepping of boundaries. In Genesis 1 everything was created to reproduce "after its kind" (Gen 1:11–12, 21, 24–25). The angelic beings are going against the will of the Creator, blurring the line between heavenly and earthly and breaching a God-given boundary.

The result of this horrible cosmic rebellion is the emergence of a creature that was never to exist, the so-called "Nephilim." These are creatures that mere humans cannot control, creatures that Israel would have to face many times. David Atkinson says that the overstepping of God-given limits "produces giants that human beings can no longer handle. It sets free powers that should have no place in this world."[5]

The sons of God taking daughters of man is the culmination of a chain of events in which people overstep boundaries. Eve and

---

5. Atkinson, *The Message of Genesis 1-11*, 131.

Adam in the Garden take the fruit of the forbidden tree; Cain kills Abel; Lamech takes two wives and celebrates vengeance.

God was sorry, says the text, and understandably so. "The Lord was sorry that He had made man on the earth, and He was grieved in His heart" (6:6). "But . . ." (v. 8). We will meet that little word again and again in the Bible. "But Noah found favor in the eyes of the Lord" (v. 8). Why Noah? Grace. The author is careful to keep things in order. "Noah found favor," then "Noah walked with God" (v. 9). The author is emphasizing the fact that Noah finds favor with God *before* he walks with God. Grace enables him to walk with God.

Old Testament scholar Alec Motyer suggests that we read Genesis 6:8 backwards. "Noah found favor/grace" becomes "Grace found Noah."[6] Grace enabled Noah to walk with God and live in intimacy with him. Grace enabled Noah to believe the strange command to build a boat in the desert with no clouds in the sky. Grace enabled Noah to throw himself on a word his contemporaries judged to be absurd.

WHAT HAPPENED IN THE FLOOD?

This leads us to the second question: "What happened in the flood?" It involved lots of water; that much is clear! But what is it that the text wants us to know?

"Blot out" is repeated three times in the story: "I will blot out man whom I have created" (6:7), "I will blot out from the face of the land every living thing that I have made" (7:4), and "Thus He blotted out . . ." (7:23). God is starting over. The same verb is also

---

6. John Goldingay, *Genesis for Everyone*, Part 1, *Chapters 1-16* (Louisville: Westminster John Knox, 2010), 98.

used in Ps 51: "blot out my transgressions" (v. 1); "blot out all my iniquities" (v. 9). It is a cry for cleansing so we can make a clean start. "I will blot out" means "I will cleanse my creation and start anew."

The cleansing is to be accomplished by removing a protective barrier. "On that same day all the fountains of the great deep burst open, and the floodgates of the sky [heavens] were opened" (7:11). After the flood subsides, we read, "The fountains of the deep and the floodgate of the sky were closed" (8:2). What is going on here? Humans have made anti-creation choices, and now they get anti-creation. Old Testament scholar Gordon Wenham explains, "In releasing the waters pent-up below and above the earth, God is undoing his great acts of separation whereby the dry land was created and the waters were confined to the seas (Gen 1:9). The earth is going back to Genesis 1:2, when waters covered its face."[7]

Boundaries have been broken by humans and angels, and judgment comes in, removing boundaries. It is awful.

The Hebrew word for "flood" is *mabbul*. It is a technical term for a part of the structure of the universe; it refers to the heavenly waters. In Hebrew thought, there were waters below the earth and above the heavens. The firmament spoken into being in Genesis 1 ("the heavens") separates these waters, the waters above from the water below. The flood involves the removal of the separating barriers. The flood is, in the words of Gerhard von Rad, "a catastrophe involving the entire cosmos."[8] The boundary is removed, and the waters break loose. Creation is allowed to sink into chaos. Humanity is given the full implications of our desires. We wanted no boundaries, and that is what we get. Awful.

---

7. Wenham, *Genesis 1-15*, 181.
8. Von Rad, *Genesis*, 124.

WHAT DOES IT MEAN FOR US NOW?

We come now to the third question: "What does it mean for us now?" We can start to answer this question by asking, "Now what? What happens after the flood?"

Grace, that is what! Unexpected, undeserved, unmerited grace, in spite of nothing changing in the human heart.

Before the flood, God saw that "the wickedness of man was great on the earth, and that every intent of the thoughts of his heart was only evil continually" (6:5). After the flood subsides, God says, "I will never again curse the ground on account of man, for the intent of man's heart is evil from his youth" (8:21). This is grace! God restores creation even though nothing in us has changed. God puts the boundary back in place simply by grace.

A number of verses in Genesis 8 tell us about how God gives grace to this fallen world. Verse 1 says, "But God remembered Noah." The verb carries with it the sense of "remember to save"; "God remembered to save Noah."[9] This verse tells us that God is not going to give up on humans. Verse 2 tells us that "God caused a wind to pass over the earth, and the water subsided." This, of course, is reminiscent of what God did "in the beginning," when the Spirit, the wind, hovered over the surface of the deep. This is also what God would do at the Red Sea, allowing his people to escape captivity (Exod 14). Here God begins again. In verse 17 God says, "Be fruitful and multiply." An expanded mandate is found in 9:1: "Be fruitful and multiply, and fill the earth." Here God renews the original creative blessing. This, once again, is grace.

---

9. Wenham believes there is a chiasm in Genesis 6-9 centering on the phrase "But God remembered Noah" (8:1). Aspects of the chiasm can be seen in the numbers used for the flood: 7, 7, 40, 150, 150, 40, 7, 7. See Wenham, *Genesis 1-15*, 156-158.

And God, giving grace upon grace (compare with John 1:16), makes a covenant, an unconditional covenant—not "I will do this for you if you do this for me," just "I will." There is no expectation placed on humanity; it is a purely unilateral covenant. This is the point of "the intent of man's heart is evil from his youth" (8:21). The covenant God makes is not determined by anything in us. It is not bound to anything we do. It is all by grace.

"Now behold" (9:9). "Behold" is a command, the imperative form of the verb "to see." "Behold!" "Look!" In the Bible the command "behold" usually introduces a surprise, an unexpected turn of events. "Now behold, I Myself do establish My covenant with you, and with your descendants after you; and with every living creature that is with you" (vv. 9–10). In the face of human sin (for Noah too is a sinner), God makes a covenant, an agreement. God makes a binding agreement with us and with every living creature, "from this day forward, for better for worse, for richer for poorer, in sickness and in health, to love and to cherish, till death do us part."[10] God makes a covenant with us while we are still sinners. Again, this is grace.

Take note of the content of the covenant. God promises to keep the earth turning, so to speak. "While the earth remains, / Seedtime and harvest, / And cold and heat, / And summer and winter, / And day and night / Shall not cease" (8:22). That is why it is appropriate that every morning we begin the day with saying, "Thank you, dear God. You are keeping your covenant."

In this covenant God also affirms the dignity of human life and sets up systems of protection. Though fallen, humans still bear the image of God (9:6), and God protects that dignity by giving

10. Traditional wedding vows as written in, e.g., *The Book of Common Prayer*, 566.

governments the authority to check human violence by the threat of consequences for violence (9:6).

The heart of the covenant is this: "All flesh shall never again be cut off by the water of the flood, neither shall there again be a flood to destroy the earth" (9:11). This is pure grace. God will keep the boundaries intact. Yes, as the story unfolds we realize that there is another cleansing to come when Jesus brings in his new heavens and new earth. But never again will God let the earth be destroyed by flood. There are times, to be sure, when it seems otherwise. When massive typhoons and hurricanes whip through parts of the earth, dumping torrents of water, it can feel like the boundary has been removed. But never again shall life be blotted out by the removal of the protective barrier.

"This is the sign of the covenant which I am making between Me and you and every living creature that is with you. . . . I set My bow in the cloud" (9:12–13). In the Old Testament, the word "bow" almost always refers to a "bow of war." "I set my bow in the cloud" in the midst of what looks like the flood coming again. In spite of human sin, God puts aside his bow, making the weapon a symbol of peace.[11] Indeed, it has become a sign of a covenant. Every time we see the bow, the rainbow, it is God saying, "Never again."

A COVENANTING GOD

This covenant, the Noahaic Covenant, is not the only covenant God makes with humanity. It is the beginning of a series of covenants.

11. Waltke and Fredricks, *Genesis*, 144.

We have been referring to Genesis 1–11 as the first half of the Bible and Genesis 12–Revelation 22 as the second half. The second half begins with another covenant, given to Abram: "I will bless you. . . . And in you [in your seed] all the families of the earth will be blessed" (vv. 2–3).

As the story continues to unfold, God makes a covenant with the children of Abraham, with Israel. Again and again God says something like, "I will take you for My people, and I will be your God" (Exod 6:7; see also, e.g., Lev 26:12; Jer 11:4; 30:22). "All I am, I give to you."

As the story continues to unfold, God makes a covenant with Israel's greatest king, David: "I will raise up your descendant [seed] after you, who will come forth from you, and I will establish his kingdom. . . . I will establish the throne of his kingdom forever" (2 Sam 7:12–13).

Then we come to the New Covenant, as God calls it, through the prophet Jeremiah. "Behold!" "Look!" "Surprise!"

> Days are coming . . . when I will make a new covenant with the house of Israel. . . . I will put My law within them and on their heart I will write it; and I will be their God, and they shall be My people. They will not teach again, each man his neighbor, and each man his brother, saying, "Know the LORD," for they will all know me, from the least of them to the greatest of them . . . for I will forgive their iniquity, and their sin I will remember no more." (Jer 31:31, 33–34)

This is the sign of the New Covenant: a loaf of bread and a cup of wine. Jesus, son of Noah, son of Abraham, son of David, seed of the woman, the new Adam, holds up a loaf of bread and cup of wine and says, "This is My body which is given for you. . . . This cup which is poured out for you is the new covenant in My blood" (Luke 22:19–20; see also Matt 26:26–28; Mark 14:22–24).

"It shall come about, when I bring a cloud over the earth, that the bow will be seen in the cloud, and I will remember My covenant" (Gen 9:14–15). God will "remember the everlasting covenant" (v. 16), not only the one with Noah, but also the one with Abraham and the one with David. And he will remember the new covenant: "I will forgive their iniquity, and their sin I will remember no more" (Jer 31:34). "And I will be [your] God, and [you] shall be My people" (Jer 31:33).

This is how the Noah part of The Story That Makes Sense of Our Stories makes sense of our stories. "I will remember my covenant." Every time we see a rainbow, we remember that God is remembering. Every time we see a loaf of bread and a cup of wine, we remember God is remembering.

If you have spent any time in the Psalms, the prayer book of Israel, you know that God's faithfulness to the covenants is what encourages and emboldens the pray-ers. Over and over again the prayers appeal to God's lovingkindness:

> "Remember O Lord, Your compassion and Your lovingkindness, /
>   For they have been from of old" (25:6).
> "How precious is Your lovingkindness, O God!" (36:7).
> "Be gracious to me, O God, according to your lovingkindness"
>   (51:1).

Sometimes the word is rendered "tender mercies": "Remember your tender mercies." In Hebrew the word is *hesed*, which means "loyalty to the covenant" or "covenant love." "Your loyalty to Your covenant has been from of old." "How precious is Your loyalty to Your covenant." "Be gracious to me according to Your loyalty to Your covenant."

After reading Jeremiah 31 and these psalms, I am moved to pray like this:

> O Lord,
> I come to you on the basis of your loyalty to your covenant.
> I do not appeal to anything in myself.
> I do not appeal to anything I have done or not done.
> I appeal to your *hesed*, to your loyalty to the covenant
> you made with me when I did not earn or deserve it.
> Write your good law in my heart.
> Give me a heart that wills what you will.
> This you promised in the covenant sealed by the blood of Jesus.
> Let me know you even as I am known by you.
> This you promised in the covenant sealed by the blood of Jesus.
> Be my God, be to me all that you are.
> Do not let me be satisfied with less than you!
> This you promised in the covenant sealed by the blood of Jesus.
> Forgive my iniquity, my twisted ways. Do not remember my sin!
> This you promised in the covenant sealed by the blood of Jesus.
> Remember your covenant, O God!

A passage from Isaiah speaks powerfully of God's covenant love:

> "For this is like the days of Noah to Me,
> When I swore that the waters of Noah
> Would not flood the earth again;
> So I have sworn that I will not be angry with you
> Nor will I rebuke you.
> "For the mountains may be removed and the hills may shake,
> But My lovingkindness will not be removed from you,
> And My covenant of peace will not be shaken,"
> Says the Lord who has compassion on you. (54:9–10)

10

God and the City

Genesis 11:1–9

We come now to the conclusion of our series of studies in Genesis 1–11, to the last chapter of what we have been calling The Story That Makes Sense of Our Stories. That is, we come now to the end of the first half of the Bible. I said in the beginning that the Bible has two halves. Yes, there are the Old Testament and the New Testament, but more essentially, there are Genesis 1–11 and Genesis 12–Revelation 22. The first half of the Bible ends with a story about God and a city, and so does the second half.

OBSERVATIONS

Let us begin with a number of observations about this passage.

"Now the whole earth used the same language and the same words" (11:1). From the larger context of the story, especially from the genealogy in Genesis 10 that sets up the story, we know that the author of Genesis is not saying that all humans spoke only one language. In recording the descendants of the three sons of Noah, the author of Genesis makes three references to different languages. Speaking of the sons of Japeth, the text says, "From these the coastlands of the nations were separated into their lands, every one according to his language, according to their families, into their nations" (10:5). Following this, the phrase "according to their languages" appears twice, referring to the descendants of Ham (v. 20) and of Shem (v. 31). In saying that the whole earth "used the same language" (11:1), the author is saying that the different people groups of Genesis 10 understood and spoke one language but had their own dialects. The situation described here is similar to the contemporary world, in which most nations can communicate in English to one degree or another even though they have their own languages.

Another important observation is that the name "Babel" originally meant "gate of the gods." This city, which is the same city as ancient Babylon, was, at the time Genesis 1–11 was written, touted as the center of the universe. Located where it was, near the intersection of the Tigris and Euphrates Rivers, it was the cradle of civilization. In this story, Babel, the gate of the gods, becomes "confusion," the new meaning of the term. The story, therefore, counters the Babylonian creation story, which says that Babylon was "founded at the time of the original creation."[1] Babylon is the gate of the gods, the way to the gods? No, it is a place of great confusion.

A third observation concerns Genesis 11:4: "Come, let us build for ourselves a city, and a tower whose top will reach into heaven." Archeologists tell us of the huge buildings called ziggurats that Babylonians and other peoples built. You have likely seen pictures of them in history or sociology textbooks or in magazines like *National Geographic*. These huge structures with tremendous

---

1. Waltke and Fredericks, *Genesis*, 180.

staircases were supposedly built so people could climb up them to the heavens. One of the most famous ziggurats was built in honor of the god Marduk in order to reach into the heavens and to make it easier for the gods to come down if they would like to do so. The name of the Marduk tower was the House of the Foundation of Heaven and Earth. Another nearby tower, in Larsa, was called the House of the Link between Heaven and Earth.[2] The building of the Tower of Babel is not just about architecture or engineering; it is fundamentally about the quest for transcendence, the desire to reach the heavens.

Our fourth observation is that the building of the tower is also an expression of the creativity the Creator has created into the human species. Like God, we are builders. A dream trip for me would be to go around the world and visit the tallest buildings of the world. Sharon and I have seen, at least from the street level, the Willis Tower, also known as the Sears Tower, in Chicago, which is 442 meters tall. I would also like to see:

The Petronas Twin Towers in Kuala Lumpur, 452 meters.
The Shanghai World Finance Centre, 492 meters.
Taipei 101 Tower, 509 meters.
One World Trade Centre in New York City, 541 meters.
Abraj Al-Bait Tower in Mecca, 601 meters.
The Burj Khalifa Tower in Dubai, 829.8 meters!

These structures are a fabulous testimony to the genius of humanity created in the image of the Creator of the universe. Just think of all the things that go into the building of such structures.

2. Ibid., 179.

A fifth observation concerns the bricks. "'Come, let us make bricks and burn them thoroughly.' And they used brick for stone, and they used tar for mortar" (v. 3). The people of Israel did not use brick or tar; they built their houses and temple with stone and mortar. Even though the Babylonians and others thought of making brick as a technological advancement, it was, to the Israelite mind, not a very wise thing to do.[3] "Come, let us make bricks and burn them thoroughly." An Israelite would think, "Boy, you *better* bake them thoroughly, or they will not hold together!" The author of Genesis calls our attention to the bricks to say that as grand as the project of tower-building was, it was built on shaky foundations. The foundational material was inherently weak. Bricks do not last long against the elements; they do not stand the test of time. The author of the story is saying that even if God had not interfered in this project, it would have one day crumbled.

Our sixth observation concerns the word "east" in verse 2: "It came about as they journeyed east, that they found a plain in Shinar [Babylon] and settled there." The text is not concerned with mere geography. In Genesis the move eastward always signals separation, moving away from something or someone. When God drives Adam and Eve out of the Garden, they move eastward (3:24). When Cain leaves the presence of God, he moves eastward (4:16). The emerging world population moving eastward shows that the population is separating itself from God. One Old Testament scholar puts it this way: "By this spatial term the narrative

3. In the Akkadian stories of tower-building, the making of bricks was celebrated by "elaborate ceremonies." See Nahum M. Sarna, *Genesis*, JPS Torah Commentary (Philadelphia: Jewish Publication Society, 1989), 82.

also conveys a metaphorical sphere, meaning the Babelites are outside God's blessing."[4]

Our seventh observation is that the Babelites are making a name for themselves. "Come, let us build for ourselves a city, and a tower whose top will reach into heaven, and let us make for ourselves a name" (v. 4). In the Bible, naming implies having a degree of dominion over what is named. In the beginning God names humans; Adam does not name himself. Then God lets Adam give names to all the animals (2:19–20).

The builders of the city and the tower want to exercise dominion for themselves. French sociologist Jacques Ellul says in his book *The Meaning of the City*, "The rebellious people are tired of being named, of being the recipient of a name. They want to name themselves."[5] This is not about wanting to gain a reputation; it is not about a quest for fame. Naming oneself is about declaring independence. The Babelites want to be independent of the God who names us.

The building of the city and the building of the tower are all about making our own world apart from God. The city, tower, and naming are all about trying to find significance and security on our own. Twice in the text we hear the word "ourselves": "Let us build for ourselves a city" and "Let us make for ourselves a name" (11:4). It is as if they are saying, "We will make life work on our own! Indeed, we are going to break through to God's realm with 'a tower whose top will reach into heaven' (v. 4)—and we are going to do it on our own."

<hr />

4. Kenneth Mathews, *Genesis 1–11:26*, The New American Commentary 1A (Nashville: Holman Reference, 1996), 478.

5. Jacques Ellul, *The Meaning of the City* (Grand Rapids: Eerdmans, 1970), 15-16.

Built on bricks, says the author of Genesis; it is all built on bricks. The quest for significance apart from God is built on bricks. The quest for security apart from God is built on bricks. The quest for immortality apart from God, for that is what the city and tower are ultimately all about, is built on bricks.

THE STRUCTURE OF THE TEXT

One final observation concerns the structure of the text itself, the way the story is put together. Like so many biblical texts, it is crafted chiastically. Rather than going in a straight line, it traces the shape of a sideways V. It moves in such a way that the major point of the story is not at the end but in the middle.

Here is how Bruce Waltke understands the chiastic structure.[6]

   A All the earth (*kol-ha'ares*) one language
      B People settle together there (*sam*)
         C Said to each other (*re'ehu*)
            D Come now, let us make bricks (*haba . . . nab la*)
               E A city and a tower
                  X And the LORD came down
               E' The city and the tower
            D' Come now.... let us confuse (*haba . . . nab la*)
         C' [Not understand] each other (*re'ehu*)
      B' People disperse from there (*sam*)
   A' Language of the whole earth (*kol-ha'ares*)

A and A' belong together —"the whole earth"
B and B' belong together—"there"
C and C' belong together—"each other"

6. Waltke and Fredricks, *Genesis*, 176.

D and D' belong together—"Come now . . . let us"
E and E' belong together—"city and tower"

It all leads to the X in the middle, to the major point: "the LORD came down" (v. 5). "'Come, let us build for ourselves a city, and a tower whose top will reach into heaven. . . .' The LORD came down to see the city and the tower" (vv. 4–5).

Do you see what the author of the story wants us to see? We build our impressive towers—100 meters, 300 meters, 500 meters, 800 meters, so very tall! But they are also so very, very small, so small that God has to leave heaven and come down to see them! This is a very humbling word.

THE MESSAGE OF THE TEXT

So, what is the Tower of Babel story saying to us city builders at this time in history? How does this part of The Story That Makes Sense of Our Stories make sense of our stories in the twenty-first century?

This story speaks to us about hubris. The last chapter of the first half of the Bible is about the divine response to human hubris, God's response to the human propensity to take life into our own hands. This story shows the divine response to the human arrogance that crosses boundaries. The God of the Bible is not opposed to cities and towers. City-ness would have eventually emerged in the Garden. As the population grew, so too the need for infrastructure: plumbing, power, transportation, housing, the moving of food supplies, the exchange of goods and services. The city is not the problem. It is the hubris in the building of cities that is the problem.

We have seen this hubris throughout our studies in Genesis 1–11 in the crossing of God-given boundaries. Adam and Eve step over a boundary and take from the tree of the knowledge of good and evil. They grab what looks like a way of being like God (3:5). Cain crosses a boundary and takes the life of his brother (4:8). Lamech crosses a boundary and takes two wives and boasts of getting revenge on a young boy who wounds him (4:23). The angels cross a boundary and take wives for themselves from the daughters of humans (6:1–2).

In building the city with a tower, humans try to cross a boundary and storm what they think are the gates of heaven. This explains God's word in 11:6: "now nothing which they purpose to do will be impossible for them." Now that they are using their technological creativity to storm heaven's gates, they will stop at nothing.

Another way to state the meaning of the Tower of Babel story is to say that there has been a change in what lies at the center—a change from the Creator to the creature, from the loving God to mere human beings. That is the problem. It is not the building of cities and towers, but the shift in center that drives the building of cities and towers. God is not offended by building cities and towers. God is not jealous of humans expressing themselves and creating structures. God's concern is that apart from him, it does not finally work.

As we have realized from the first chapter of the first half of the Bible, we were made in such a way that human existence and human security only work if the Creator is the center. No other center is big enough or strong enough to hold it all together. This explains the strange words the city builders say at the end of their speech: "Come, let us build for ourselves a city, and a tower whose top will reach into heaven, and let us make for ourselves a name, otherwise we will be scattered abroad over the face of the whole earth" (v. 4). "Otherwise we will be scattered." They are in some way feeling the consequences of the shift in center. Even in their one common language and one common effort to build a tower and make a name, they feel insecure; they sense it is not really working.

Helmut Thielicke is the one who helped me see this. In his book *How the World Began*, he says,

> Perhaps some of you have already noted a passage that crops up, somewhat hiddenly and enigmatically, at the very beginning of our story: "Let us build ourselves a city, and a tower with its top in the heavens . . . lest we be scattered abroad upon the face of the whole earth." Hence, long before the judgment of dispersion fell upon them, men already had a premonition, a dim fear that they might break apart and that even their languages might be confused. They sensed the hidden presence of centrifugal, dispersive forces.
>
> This arises from the fact that they have suffered something that might be called the "loss of a center" and that now that they have banished God from their midst they no longer have anything that binds them to each other. Always the trend is the same: wherever God has been deposed, some substitute point has to be created to bind people together in some fashion or other. You start a war, perhaps, in order to divert attention from internal political dissensions and thus create a new solidarity by making people feel that they are facing a common threat. Or you build a tower of Babel in order to concentrate people's attention upon a new center by rallying them to united and enthusiastic effort and this way pull together the dispersive elements. Or you whip together by terror those who will not stay together voluntarily. Or you utilize the powers of suggestion, "propaganda," and "ideology," in order to generate the feeling of community by means of psychological tricks and thus make people want precisely what you want them to want.
>
> All of these are substitute ties, conclusive attempts to replace the lost center with a synthetic center. But this attempt—this *experimentum medietatis*—is doomed to failure. The centrifugal forces

go on pulling and rending and a hidden time-fuse is ticking in the piers of all the bridges.[7]

A hidden time fuse is ticking in the piers of all the bridges. Thielicke continues,

> In a society which has lost its center and consists of not much more than interest groups, employers' associations and labor unions, tenants' and home-owners' associations—we call it a "pluralistic society," without realizing the fateful Babylonian curse that lies behind this pluralism!—in such a society fear and distrust prevail, precisely the centrifugal forces which exploded with a vengeance at the tower of Babel.
>
> Do we understand now that this story is something like a compendium of what we experience every day in ourselves and all around us? For a moment God opens the armored strongbox and lets us see the secret survey map of the course of the world.
>
> At all events it no longer requires a thunderbolt from heaven to drive men apart. Since they have become godless the ferments of decay and disintegration are at work everywhere even without a blast from heaven.[8]

Though written in 1949, this is true of every era.

Again, we see that judgment is always God simply giving us the full implications of the path we have chosen for ourselves. The story of the Tower of Babel tells us that the centrifugal forces set in motion by the shift in center pulls us apart. David Atkinson points out that "if you will live without God as the centre, you will have no centre at all."[9]

---

7. Thielicke, *How the World Began*, 280-281.
8. Ibid., 284.
9. Atkinson, *The Message of Genesis 1-11*, 182.

And so God lets the centrifugal forces have their way. God confuses the one language. Babel, the "gate to the gods," becomes Babel, "confusion." God does it to keep us from further assault on reality, to keep us from ruining our lives on the path of "naming ourselves" in independence from God.

And God scatters the people "abroad over the face of the whole earth" (v. 9). The story ends. The tower is not finished, the city is half-built, and the story just ends.

THE END OF THE STORY?

As we have made our way through Genesis 1–11, you may have detected a pattern to the stories. The stories repeat the same cycle: grace, rebellion, judgment, new grace. God comes in grace. Humanity rebels in some way. They receive the judgment about which humanity was warned. And then, unexpectedly, God offers new grace to the rebelling and undeserving humanity. Grace, rebellion, judgment, new grace.

In the story of Adam and Eve, God acts in grace when he calls humans into being and gives them everything they need to be "fully human and fully alive." But they begin to believe the serpent's twisting of God's word, and they become suspicious that God is withholding something they need. So they rebel, deciding to take life into their own hands, living independently of God. Then comes judgment, just as God said it would. Life begins to unravel, paradise is lost, and the Garden becomes a cemetery. And then God offers new grace. Adam and Eve remain alive in spite of the threat of death. God clothes the shame-filled naked rebels. And he makes a promise that one day a seed of the woman will come and crush the head of the serpent. Grace, rebellion, judgment, new grace.

In the story of Cain and Abel, God, in an act of grace, gives Cain a brother. Cain rebels and murders Abel, and then he runs off to make a city where he thinks he will not have to deal with God. And then there is new grace: God graciously establishes a protective relationship between God and Cain, and God enables the rebel to build a city to provide for his family. Grace, rebellion, judgment, new grace.

In the flood story, even though God graciously gives humanity all that is needed as the avalanche of sin continues, humanity again rebels at even deeper levels. Angels rebel. Society grows more and more decadent. God responds by cleansing creation with a huge flood, caused by the removal of a protective barrier. Then there is new grace. God spares the life of Noah and his family, and through Noah he begins to re-people the earth. Grace, rebellion, judgment, new grace. "Where sin increased, grace abounded all the more" (Rom 5:20)!

Then there is the Tower of Babel. Due to the grace of God, humans are given the capacity to create. Humanity rebels. God responds in judgment, scattering the builders and frustrating their attempt to build a human-centered civilization. And then the story ends. Grace, rebellion, judgment. Period. No new grace. The nations are scattered over the face of the globe, alienated from each other, arguing over boundary lines, wrestling with access to natural resources, always preparing for war. Grace, rebellion, judgment. The end. No new grace.

Is that it? It cannot end there, can it, Lord? "Is God's gracious forbearance now exhausted?"[10] God forbid!

At this point the camera turns from its panoramic sweeps of the scattered nations and narrows its focus to one couple in one of the nations. It is stunning. All the nations are scattered over the globe, still rebelling, still under the judgment, still suffering the

---

10. Von Rad and Marks, *Genesis*, 149.

inherent consequences of their "no center" way of life. And then the camera slowly zooms in on an elderly couple living in Ur of the Chaldeans, in what is now Iraq. The two people are named Abram and Sarai, later to be renamed Abraham and Sarah. Early in the story of this couple, the text says,

> Now the LORD said to Abram,
> "Go forth from your country,
> And from your relatives
> And from your father's house,
> To the land which I will show you;
> And I will make you a great nation,
> And I will bless you,
> And make your name great;
> And so you shall be a blessing;
> And I will bless those who bless you,
> And the one who curses you I will curse.
> And in you all the families of the earth will be blessed." (Gen 12:1–3)

What is going on here? Simply and profoundly this: God is providing new grace for the city. God's call on Abram and Sarai of Iraq is God's new grace for all the cities of all the nations scattered over the face of the earth. "I will make your name great" (v. 2). All that the Babelites wanted to achieve by making a name for themselves on their own, God will do. God will rebuild the fallen world. God will build the city we seek.

The first half of the Bible ends with judgment. The second half of the Bible begins with new grace. The cycle is not broken. Grace, rebellion, judgment, new grace. "In you all the families of the earth will be blessed" (v. 3).

THE END OF THE STORY!

It takes some time for the new grace to unfold—around two thousand years!— but finally the camera zooms in on another couple of the line of Abraham and Sarah, this time in Bethlehem of Judea. The shot shows us Joseph and Mary and finally just Mary, who is a virgin, unable to conceive on her own. This is the same note on which Genesis 11 ends. "Sarai was barren; she had no child" (v. 30). God's work of new grace for the city begins through a barren line, a humanly helpless line. Abraham and Sarah try to get pregnant for twenty-five years without success. And then, well past Sarai's age of childbearing, God gives grace to conceive. So are we surprised that when the long process finally comes to its climax, we meet a virgin?

That is the way it is with grace. God comes to do his new work when we finally realize that we are not able to do it. "Let us make for ourselves a name" (11:4). No! "I will make your name great" (12:2).

The descendant of Abraham and Sarah conceives. A virgin conceives! And she gives birth to a Son, to the seed of the woman promised in the Garden, the one in whom all the peoples, all the nations of the world will be blessed.

But who is this seed? Who is this Son? Who is this Jesus?

Let us return to the structure of the closing story of the first half of the Bible. It is crafted to focus on "the LORD came down" (11:5). The Lord did come down, much further down than the Babelites realized, much further down than the author of Genesis realized. The Lord came all the way down. The divine response to human hubris is divine humanity. The Lord came all the way down. Jesus is the Lord-come-down!

In him the city finds its center, its true center. In him we find our significance and security. In him we find our unity. In Jesus we find all we are longing for in building our cities and towers. We need not construct towers to take us into heaven. Heaven came to us. Heaven came down, all the way down.

And because we can now live around the true center, the judgment of Babel can be lifted. Confusion can be removed. Fifty days after he rises from the grave, Jesus pours out his Spirit upon the newly formed community centered on him (Acts 2), and people from all over the world hear the good news spoken simultaneously in their own languages. Pentecost is the reversal of the judgment of Babel.

"The LORD came down," all the way down, bringing new grace to the city.

One day there will be another "came down." He who came down will come again. The end of the second half of the Bible tells us about it: "And I saw the holy city, new Jerusalem, coming down out of heaven from God, made ready as a bride adorned for her husband" (Rev 21:2). "Then he showed me a river of the water of life, clear as crystal, coming from the throne of God and of the Lamb, in the middle of its street. On either side of the river was the tree of life. . . . There will no longer be any curse. . . . They will see His face, and His name will be on their foreheads" (Rev 22:1–4).

It is for that city that we city builders were created. It is that city that Jesus-the-center calls us to seek, as did Abraham: "for he was looking for the city which has foundations [not bricks!], whose architect and builder is God" (Heb 11:10).

The cycle did not break. Grace, rebellion, judgment, new grace. Jesus of Nazareth. "The LORD came down." He is the new grace for the city.

Questions for Small-Group Studies

Chapter 1: The Creator Creates Creation

1. When you hear the word "creation," what do you think of?

   When you hear the word, how do you feel?

2. How does Genesis 1 connect with your culture's attempt to make sense of reality?

3. How does it correct the culture's sense of reality?

4. How would life be different if people believed "Creator creates creation"?

5. For prayer:

   > Creator God, maker of all that is:
   > in creation we see the glorious outworking of your imagination.
   > Every creature, through your life-giving Spirit,
   > is spoken into existence and loved into eternity.
   > For the gift of life we praise and thank you.
   >
   > Generous God, giver of all good things;
   > in your Son we see the wonder and the cost of love.
   > In his living and dying we feel your compassion
   > and see your purpose. In his glorious resurrection
   > we know death not only as ending but as beginnings.

For the promise of life eternal we praise and thank
you.

Life-giving God, by your Spirit
you brought creation out of chaos and gave life to the
world.
Now you sustain all things and still you give life to
the lifeless.
You have found us and changed us, awoken us and
inspired us.

You have given us new life in Jesus Christ:
you have wooed us in love and created love within
us.

God our creator, redeemer and sustainer,
we give you thanks and praise.[1]

6. For further reflection, consider the following passage
from Chapter 1: "The universe is not an accident, and
you are not an accident. There is a Creator, a Person, one
as personal as you and me. This Creator, who delights to
create, created you and everything around you. This Creator, who delights to create, created you and everything
around you." Do you really believe this?

Chapter 2: The Glory of Being Human

1. If someone asked you what it means to be human, how
would you answer?

1. Christopher Ellis and Myra Blyth, eds., *Gathering for Worship:
Patterns and Prayers for the Community of Disciples* (Norwich, U.K.: Canterbury, 2005), 325.

2. How does Richard Bube's explanation of levels of meaning help us understand creation?

3. How should people act as those who bear God's image?

4. What does it mean that we were made in the image and likeness of a God who is a relational being?

5. What does Genesis 1 teach us about Sabbath and rest?

6. For prayer:

> At the beginning of time and space, God gave us a world.
> And God filled it with the useful—
> with granite, with gravity, with grapes.
> And God gave us minds and hands to engineer the granite,
> to probe the forces of gravity, to squeeze the grapes.
> At the beginning of time and space, God gave us a world.
> And God filled it with the beautiful—
> with marble, with molds, with marigolds.
> And God gave us compassion and imagination
> to shape the marble into sculptures, the molds into medicines,
> the marigolds into tapestries of yellow and bronze.
> At the beginning of time and space, God gave us a world.
> And God filled it with the comic—
> with croaking bullfrogs, with the buoyancy of water,
> with duck-billed platypuses.
> And God gave us, as image-bearers of God,
> a sense of humor and different ways of seeing

in order to delight in the world.
At the beginning of time and space, God gave us a
world.
And God filled it with mystery—
with living cells and dying stars,
with black holes and the speed of light,
with human beings.
And God gave us dominion over the earth,
to till it and to nurture it with curiosity and creativity.
At the beginning of time, God gave us a world.
Let us give praise and thanksgiving to God, our
Creator.[2]

7. For further reflection: As you go through this week, practice seeing others as those made in the image and likeness of God. How does this change how you treat them?

Chapter 3: Fourfold Relational Harmony

1. Describe the most holy person that you can think of. How important is relationality to your description of this person?

2. After reading this chapter, how would you say your relationship with the earth (including the materiality of your body) is? Is there anything you need to change in this relationship?

3. How is your relationship with others? After reading this

2. Emily R. Brink and John D. Witvliet, eds., *The Worship Sourcebook* (Grand Rapids: Faith Alive, 2004), 377.

chapter, is there anything you need to change in this area?

4. What does it mean to have a good relationship with yourself? What does that look like?

5. Relationship with God includes accountability and intimacy. Do you need to experience one of these more deeply this week?

6. For prayer:

> God of love and justice,
> we long for peace within and peace without.
> We long for harmony in our families,
> for serenity in the midst of struggle.
> We long for the day when our homes
> will be a dwelling place for your love.
> Yet we confess that we are often anxious,
> we do not trust each other,
> and we harbor violence.
> We are not willing to take the risks
> and make the sacrifices that love requires.
> Look upon us with kindness and grace.
> Rule in our homes and in all the world;
> show us how to walk in your paths,
> through the mercy of our Savior. Amen.[3]

7. For further reflection: What would shalom look like in the relationships I have? What would I need to do to experience more shalom in my life?

---

3. Ibid., 101.

Chapter 4: Only One Command

1. Describe the first time you remember disobeying something your parents told you to do.

2. This chapter gives a number of clarifications about what God is after in this command. Which of the clarifications was most life-giving to you? Do you struggle to understand or accept any of the clarifications?

3. What is "the knowledge of good and evil"?

4. What was the "only one command" that God gave in the garden?

5. For prayer:

    > God of grace,
    > in your love and compassion
    > strengthen our faith
    > and enliven our hope.
    > God of grace,
    > by your Spirit's breath
    > help us to pray
    > and to trust you
    > now and every day,
    > through Jesus Christ our Lord. Amen.[4]

6. For further reflection: Where is God calling me to trust him (or trust him again or trust him more) this week?

4. Ellis and Blyth, *Gathering for Worship*, 268.

Chapter 5: Messing with Our Minds

1. How was Satan pictured in the culture you grew up in? In what ways does this differ from the portrayal of him in Genesis 3?

2. Review the three steps that Satan takes in tempting Eve. Can you describe how he uses the same steps with you?

3. Eve ends up twisting and misquoting God's words. Relate a time when you have discovered that you had been doing that.

4. What does Genesis 3 reveal about sin?

5. For prayer:

> Gracious God,
> our sins are too heavy to carry,
> too real to hide,
> and too deep to undo.
> Forgive what our lips tremble to name,
> what our hearts can no longer bear,
> and what has become for us
> a consuming fire of judgment.
> Set us free from a past that we cannot change;
> open to us a future in which we can be changed;
> and grant us grace
> to grow more and more in your likeness and image;
> through Jesus Christ, the light of the world. Amen.[5]

5. Brink and Witvliet, *The Worship Sourcebook*, 91.

6. For further reflection: In what ways do I relate to God with suspicion and distrust in my daily life?

Chapter 6: Grace Outruns the Avalanche

1. Have you ever experienced an avalanche or mudslide, or seen the results of one? Describe it.

2. How does the sin in the garden affect the four primary relationships?

3. How was grace experienced in these four primary relationships after the sin?

4. What is the proto-gospel revealed in this chapter?

5. For prayer:

> O Jesus, light of the world,
> come into the dark places of this earth.
> You bring a light from God that only you can shed.
> Light eternal, your light shines in the darkness,
> and the darkness does not overcome it.
> We bring to you the darkness of our world
> in war, starvation, cruelty, and exploitation.
> We bring to you the darkness of our earth,
> damaged and defaced by pollution.
> We bring to you the darkness of our nation,
> beset with conflict of race and class, religion and politics.
> We bring to you the darkness of our relationships,
> people not looking, not speaking, not listening, not forgiving.
> We bring to you the darkness of our own souls,

hidden closets we have not visited or cleaned out for
years.
O Jesus, light of the world, be a morning star above
for us,
a radiance within, the shining all around that lets us
live in love.
Only then shall we be reflectors of your brightness
and give glory to God in heaven. Amen.[6]

6. For further reflection: As you go through this week,
   notice areas of brokenness in and around you. Where are
   you seeing hints of grace in the midst of the darkness?

Chapter 7: Grace Outside the Garden

1. Do you have any siblings? Describe your relationship
   with them.

2. How is grace for the city shown in this chapter?

3. Why was God pleased with Abel and his sacrifice and not
   with Cain and his?

4. Read Luke 10:25–37. How does Jesus' answer to the question "Who is my neighbor?" affect our understanding of
   "Where is my brother?"

5. For prayer:

   > O Lord, though you were rich,
   > for our sakes you became poor.
   > You have promised in your gospel

6. Ibid., 507.

that whatever is done to the least,
you will receive as done to you.
Give us grace, we humbly ask you,
to be ever willing and ready to minister, as you enable us,
to the necessities of our brothers and sisters,
and to extend the blessings of your kingdom
over all the world, to your praise and glory,
God over all, blessed forever. Amen.[7]

6.   For further reflection: Think of three of the faces you have seen this week, asking, "Where is my sister?" or "Where is my brother?" in relation to these people.

Chapter 8: Keeping His Word

1.   How far back can you trace your family tree? How important is knowing your ancestry to you?

2.   What do biblical genealogies teach us?

3.   Choose one of the four key words that this chapter highlights from Genesis 5 ("begat," "died," "rest," "took"). What did you learn from its discussion of one of these words?

4.   Discuss this Ravi Zacharias quote: "Jesus did not come into this world to make bad people good. He came into this world to make dead people live."[8]

5.   For prayer:

7. Ibid., 653.
8. Zacharias, *Cries of The Heart*, 112.

Lord, you have been our dwelling place
in all generations.
Before the mountains were brought forth,
or you had formed the earth and the world,
from everlasting to everlasting you are God.
Teach us, Lord, to count our days
that we may gain a wise heart.
Satisfy us in the morning with your steadfast love,
so that we may rejoice and be glad all our days.
Through Christ, our Lord. Amen.[9]

6. For further reflection: Choose one of Jonathan Edward's resolutions to read over every morning. Does it change how you live your day?

Chapter 9: Starting Over

1. Have you ever been in a flood? If so, describe what it was like. If not, describe a flood that you recall seeing on the news.

2. What does the fact that other cultures have flood stories say to you about the biblical story?

3. Why did the flood happen? What does this reveal about God's character?

4. What surprises you about this part of The Story That Makes Sense of Our Stories?

9. Brink and Witvliet, *The Worship Sourcebook*, 543 (based on Ps 91).

5. For prayer:

> O LORD,
> I come to you on the basis of your loyalty to your covenant.
> I do not appeal to anything in myself.
> I do not appeal to anything I have done or not done.
> I appeal to your *hesed*, to your loyalty to the covenant you made with me when I did not earn or deserve it.
> Write your good law in my heart.
> Give me a heart that wills what you will.
> This you promised in the covenant sealed by the blood of Jesus.
> Let me know you even as I am known by you.
> This you promised in the covenant sealed by the blood of Jesus.
> Be my God; be to me all that you are.
> Do not let me be satisfied with less than you!
> This you promised in the covenant sealed by the blood of Jesus.
> Forgive my iniquity, my twisted ways. Do not re-member my sin!
> This You promised in the covenant sealed by the blood of Jesus.
> Remember your covenant, O God!

6. For further reflection: Look for a rainbow this week. What does it remind you about God's faithfulness?

Chapter 10: God and the City

1. What does "hubris" mean? Give some examples from your own life, from history, or from literature.

2. The chapter starts by making seven observations about the text. Which observation "grabbed" you?

3. What does the structure of the text show us about what we should learn from the Tower of Babel?

4. How does The Story That Makes Sense of Our Stories end? What does that teach us about our stories?

5. For prayer:

> Our cities cry to you, O God, from out their pain and strife;
> you made us for yourself alone, but we choose empty life.
> Our goals are pleasure, gold, and power; injustice stalks our earth;
> in vain we seek for rest, for joy, for sense of human worth.

> Yet still you walk our streets, O Christ! We know Your presence here,
> where humble Christians love and serve in godly grace and fear.
> O Word made flesh, be seen in us! May all we say and do
> affirm you God incarnate still and turn sad hearts to you!

> Your people are your hands and feet to serve your world today;
> our lives, the book our cities read to help them find your way.
> O pour your sovereign Spirit out on heart and will

and brain:
inspire your church with love and power to ease our
cities' pain!

O healing Saviour, Prince of Peace, salvation's source
and sum,
for You our broken cities cry—O come, Lord Jesus,
come!
With truth your royal diadem, with righteousness
your rod,
O come, Lord Jesus, bring to earth the city of our
God![10]

6. For further reflection: Take a field trip to look at the tallest (or most impressive) buildings in your town or city. What do you think the builders were trying to say? What do you think God would want to say to them?

10. Margaret Clarkson, "Our Cities Cry to You, O God," altered by Hope Publishing Company, in *Common Praise*, #591 (Toronto: Anglican Book Centre, 2000).

Bibliography

Atkinson, David J. *The Message of Genesis 1–11*. Leicester, U.K.: IVP Academic, 1990.

Bailey, Kenneth E. *Paul Through Mediterranean Eyes: Cultural Studies in 1 Corinthians*. Downers Grove, Ill.: InterVarsity, 2011.

Barclay, William. *The Letter to the Hebrews*. Edinburgh: Saint Andrew, 1955.

Barth, Karl. *Church Dogmatics 3/2: The Doctrine of Creation*. Edited by G. W. Bromiley and T. F. Torrance. Translated by J. W. Edwards, O. Bussey, and H. Knight. Edinburgh: T&T Clark, 1958.

Bauckham, Richard. T*he Bible and Ecology: Rediscovering the Community of Creation*. Waco, Tex.: Baylor University Press, 2010.

Boice, James Montgomery. *Philippians: An Expositional Commentary*. Grand Rapids: Zondervan, 1971.

Bonhoeffer, Dietrich. *Creation and Fall: A Theological Interpretation of Genesis 1–3*. Revised by the editorial staff of SCM Press. Translated by John C. Fletcher. New York: Macmillan, 1959

The Book of Common Prayer and Adminisrtration of the Sacraments [. . .]. Toronto: Anglican Book Centre, 1962.

Brink, Emily R., and John D. Witvliet, eds. *The Worship Sourcebook*. Grand Rapids: Faith Alive, 2004.

Brown, Francis, S. R. Driver, and Charles A. Briggs. *The New Brown-Driver-Briggs-Gesenius Hebrew English Lexicon*. Peabody, Mass.: Hendrickson, 1979.

Bruce, F. F. *The Epistle to the Hebrews*. Grand Rapids: Eerdmans, 1964.

Brueggemann, Walter. *Genesis*. Interpretation: A Bible Commentary for Teaching and Preaching. Atlanta: John Knox, 1982.

———. *Theology of the Old Testament*. Minneapolis: Augsburg Fortress, 1997.

Bube, Richard H. *The Human Quest: A New Look at Science and the Christian Faith*. Waco, Tex.: Word, 1971.

Chesterton, G. K. *Orthodoxy*. Vancouver, B.C.: Regent College Publishing, 2004.

Clarkson, Margaret. "Our Cities Cry to You, O God." Altered by Hope Publishing Company. In *Common Praise*, #591. Toronto: Anglican Book Centre, 2000.

Crouch, Andy. *Playing God: Redeeming the Gift of Power*. Downers Grove, Ill.: IVP, 2013.

Dunn, James D. G. *Christology in the Making: A New Testament Inquiry into the Origins of the Doctrine of the Incarnation*. Philadelphia: Westminster, 1980.

Dylan, Bob. "Man Gave Names to All the Animals." *Slow Train Coming*. Columbia MOVLP1459, 1979, LP.

Edwards, Jonathan. *The Works of Jonathan Edwards*. Vol. 16, *Letters and Personal Writings*. Edited by George S. Claghorn. New Haven, Conn.: Yale University Press, 1998.

Ellis, Christopher, and Myra Blyth, eds. *Gathering for Worship: Patterns and Prayers for the Community of Disciples*. Norwich, U.K.: Canterbury, 2005.

Ellul, Jacques. *The Meaning of the City*. Grand Rapids: Eerdmans, 1970.

Fromm, Erich. *Escape from Freedom*. New York: Farrar & Rinehart, 1941.

Fuller, Daniel P. "The Unity of the Bible." Unpublished lecture notes for "Hermeneutics," taught at Fuller Theology Seminary, winter semester 1970.

―――. *The Unity of the Bible: Unfolding God's Plan for Humanity.* Grand Rapids: Zondervan, 1992.

Goldingay, John. *Genesis for Everyone.* Part 1, *Chapters 1–16.* Louisville: Westminster John Knox, 2010.

Greidanus, Sidney. *Preaching Christ from Genesis: Foundations for Expository Sermons.* Grand Rapids: Eerdmans, 2007.

Hart, Ian. "Genesis 1:1–2:3 as a Prologue to the Book of Genesis." *Tyndale Bulletin* 46/2 (1995): 315–336.

Henry, Matthew. *Commentary on the Whole Bible: Genesis to Revelation.* Edited by Leslie F. Church. Grand Rapids: Zondervan, 1961.

Irenaeus. *Against Heresies.* In *The Ante-Nicene Fathers: Translations of the Fathers Down to A.D. 325,* Vol. 1, edited by Alexander Roberts and James Donaldson and revised by A. Cleveland Coxe, 309–567. American repr. of the Edinburgh ed. Repr., Edinburgh, T&T Clark; Grand Rapids: Eerdmans, 1989.

Jones, E. Stanley. *Abundant Living.* Nashville: Abingdon, 1942.

Kidner, Derek. *Genesis: An Introduction and Commentary.* Tyndale Old Testament Commentary Series. Downers Grove, Ill.: Tyndale, 1967.

Kitchen, Kenneth Anderson. *The Bible in Its World: The Bible and Archaeology Today.* Downers Grove, Ill.: InterVarsity, 1977.

Kline, Meredith G. "Genesis." In *The New Bible Commentary,* edited by D. Guthrie and J. A. Motyer, 79–114. Grand Rapids: Eerdmans, 1970.

Leibniz, Gottfried W. *Theodicy.* Translated by E. M. Huggard. Don Mills, Ont.: J. M. Dent & Sons, 1966.

L'Engle, Madeleine. *And It Was Good: Reflections on Beginnings.* Wheaton, Ill.: H. Shaw, 1983.

Lewis, C. S.*The Screwtape Letters and Screwtape Proposes a Toast.* New York: Macmillan, 1961.

———. *The Weight of Glory.* San Francisco: HarperCollins, 1976.

Lovelace, Richard F. *Dynamics of Spiritual Life.* Downers Grove, Ill.: InterVarsity, 1979.

Luther, Martin. *Luther's Works*, Vol. 1, *Lectures on Genesis Chapters 1–5.* Edited by Jaroslav Pelikan. Translated by George V. Schick. Saint Louis: Concordia, 1958.

Mathews, Kenneth. *Genesis 1–11:26.* The New American Commentary 1A. Nashville: Holman Reference, 1996.

Naisbitt, John, and Patricia Aburdene. *Megatrends 2000: Ten New Directions for the 1990's.* New York: William Morrow, 1990.

The Passion of the Christ. Directed by Mel Gibson. Santa Monica: Icon Productions, 2004.

Piper, John. "The Fatal Disobedience of Adam and the Triumphant Obedience of Christ." Desiring God. August 26, 2007. <http://www.desiringgod.org/messages/the-fatal-disobedience-of-adam-and-the-triumphant-obedience-of-christ.>

———. "The Image of God: An Approach from Biblical and Systematic Theology." *Studia Biblica et Theologica* 1/1 (1971): 15–32.

Powell, John. *Fully Human, Fully Alive: A New Life Through a New Vision.* Niles, Ill.: Argus, 1976.

Provan, Iain. *Seriously Dangerous Religion: What the Old Testament Really Says and Why It Matters.* Waco, Tex.: Baylor University Press, 2014.

Rad, Gerhard von. *Genesis: A Commentary.* Translated by John H. Marks. Philadelphia: Westminster, 1961.

———. *Old Testament Theology.* Vol. 2, *The Theology of Israel's Prophetic Traditions.* Translated by D. M. G. Stalker. New York: Harper & Row, 1962.

"Reason for Quitting Christianity." Anne Rice: The Official Site. Accessed September 12, 2017. <http://www.annerice.com/Chamber-Christianity.html.>

Rice, Anne. *Christ The Lord: Out of Egypt.* New York: Knopf, 2005.

———. *Christ the Lord: The Road to Cana.* New York: Knopf, 2008.

Richards, Larry. *Let Day Begin: Studies in Genesis and Job.* Bible Alive Series. Elgin, Ill.: David C. Cook, 1976.

Rijn, Rembrandt Harmenszoon van. *Return of the Prodigal Son.* C. 1661–1669. Oil on canvas. 262 cm x 205 cm. Hermitage Museum, St. Petersburg, Russia.

Rodgers, Richard, and Oscar Hammerstein II. "Do-Re-Mi." In *The Sound of Music.* Rodgers and Hammerstein, 1959.

Sarna, Nahum M. *Genesis.* JPS Torah Commentary. Philadelphia: Jewish Publication Society, 1989.

Schaeffer, Francis A. *Genesis in Space and Time: The Flow of Biblical History.* Downers Grove, Ill.: InterVarsity, 1972.

Shepherd, J. Barrie. *Encounters: Poetic Meditations on the Old Testament.* New York: Pilgrim, 1983.

Simon and Garfunkel. "I Am a Rock." Written by Paul Simon. *Sounds of Silence.* CBS WKCS 9269, 1965, LP.

Smedes, Lewis B. *Sex for Christians: The Limits and Liberties of Sexual Living.* Grand Rapids: Eerdmans, 1976.

Thielicke, Helmut. *How the World Began: Man in the First Chapters of the Bible.* Translated by John W. Doberstein. Philadelphia: Fortress, 1961.

Wallace, Ronald. *The Ten Commandments: A Study of Ethical Freedom.* Eugene, Ore.: Wipf & Stock, 1998.

Waltke, Bruce K., and Cathi J. Fredricks. *Genesis: A Commentary.* Grand Rapids: Zondervan, 2001.

Walton, John H. *The Lost World of Genesis One: Ancient Cosmology and the Origins Debate.* Downers Grove, Ill.: IVP Academic, 2009.

Wenham, Gordon J. *Genesis 1–15.* Word Biblical Commentary 1. Waco, Tex.: Word, 1987.

Willard, Dallas. *The Spirit of the Disciplines: Understanding How God Changes Lives.* 1988. Paperback ed., New York: Harper-Collins, 1991.

Wright, Christopher J. H. *The Mission of God: Unlocking The Bible's Grand Narrative.* Downers Grove, Ill.: InterVarsity, 2006.

Zacharias, Ravi. *Cries of The Heart: Bringing God Near When He Feels So Far.* Nashville: Word, 1998.

For Further Reading

The footnotes and bibliography of this book will show you some of the resources that I have used in my study of Genesis. For further reading, I especially commend the following resources:

Atkinson, David J. *The Message of Genesis 1–11*. Leicester, U.K.: IVP Academic, 1990.

Bonhoeffer, Dietrich. *Creation and Fall: A Theological Interpretation of Genesis 1–3*. Revised by the editorial staff of SCM Press. Translated by John C. Fletcher. New York: Macmillan, 1959.

Brueggemann, Walter. *Genesis*. Interpretation: A Bible Commentary for Teaching and Preaching. Atlanta: John Knox, 1982.

Kidner, Derek. *Genesis: An Introduction and Commentary*. Tyndale Old Testament Commentary Series. Downers Grove, Ill.: Tyndale, 1967.

Provan, Iain. *Seriously Dangerous Religion: What the Old Testament Really Says and Why It Matters*. Waco, Tex.: Baylor University Press, 2014.

Rad, Gerhard von. *Genesis: A Commentary*. Translated by John H. Marks. Philadelphia: Westminster, 1961.

Schaeffer, Francis A. *Genesis in Space and Time: The Flow of Biblical History*. Downers Grove, Ill.: InterVarsity, 1972.

Thielicke, Helmut. *How the World Began: Man in the First Chapters of the Bible*. Translated by John W. Doberstein. Philadelphia: Fortress, 1961.

Waltke, Bruce K., and Cathi J. Fredricks. *Genesis: A Commentary*. Grand Rapids: Zondervan, 2001.

Walton, John H. *The Lost World of Genesis One: Ancient Cosmology and the Origins Debate*. Downers Grove, Ill.: IVP Academic, 2009.

Acknowledgements

So many people have helped me in the preparation of this book. Carolyn Vanderberg, serving as my assistant at First Baptist, Vancouver, turned my hand-written notes into typed copy. Then Doug Hills-Liao, following Carolyn as my assistant, put the notes together in book form, and helped with the Small Group questions. Regent graduates Brent Siemens and Oliver Hung (now serving me as my assistant) went through the manuscript with a fine-tooth comb, raising very important questions and suggesting ways to put things more correctly. David Doherty was an excellent copyeditor. Thanks to Robert Hand for managing the publication process and for the cover and interior design. And Bill Reimer, a friend who believes in me, and has worked so hard to make the heart of my preaching and teaching more widely accessible. To each of them I express my profound gratitude.

Two people helped me the most: Daniel Payton Fuller, Professor Emeritus of Hermeneutics at Fuller Theological Seminary, under whom I had the matchless privilege of studying from 1969 to 1973, and my wife, Sharon, who has listened to me teach the material in many different venues (in the US, Canada, and the Philippines), raising questions and adding her perspective as one who works with children. She "sees" in ways I do not. I do not know where I would be without her partnership. To her the book is dedicated with all my love.

CPSIA information can be obtained
at www.ICGtesting.com
Printed in the USA
LVHW092230240519
619085LV00001B/20/P

9 781573 835695